WILLARD A. PALMER MORTON MANUS AMANDA VICK LETHCO

INSTRUCTIONS for USE

1. The student beginning Lesson Book 2 of Alfred's Basic Adult Piano Course should receive this book at the same time. The first assignment is made with the first piece in the Lesson Book. Subsequent assignments are made according to the instructions in the upper right hand corner of each page of the THEORY BOOK, which is coordinated with the LESSON BOOK, page by page.
2. Every concept introduced in the Lesson Book is reviewed and reinforced in this Theory Book. These drills will insure that the student understands every principle and idea as it is presented, and will review all of the concepts introduced in earlier lessons.
3. All theory lessons should be completed by the student AT HOME, then checked and discussed by the teacher at the next lesson.

© Copyright MCMLXXXV by Alfred Publishing Co., Inc.

All rights reserved. Printed in USA.

Assign with the beginning of ADULT LESSON BOOK 2.

Review—The Key of C Major

KEY SIGNATURE: NO SHARPS, NO FLATS

REMEMBER: When moving from one chord to another it usually sounds best to keep a COMMON TONE between neighboring chords, to make a smooth progression.

In THEORY BOOK ONE, you learned that you can move from the root position of the I CHORD of any MAJOR KEY by keeping the lowest note as a COMMON TONE between **I & IV**, and the highest note as a COMMON TONE betwen **I & V7**.

In the KEY OF C MAJOR, this works as follows:

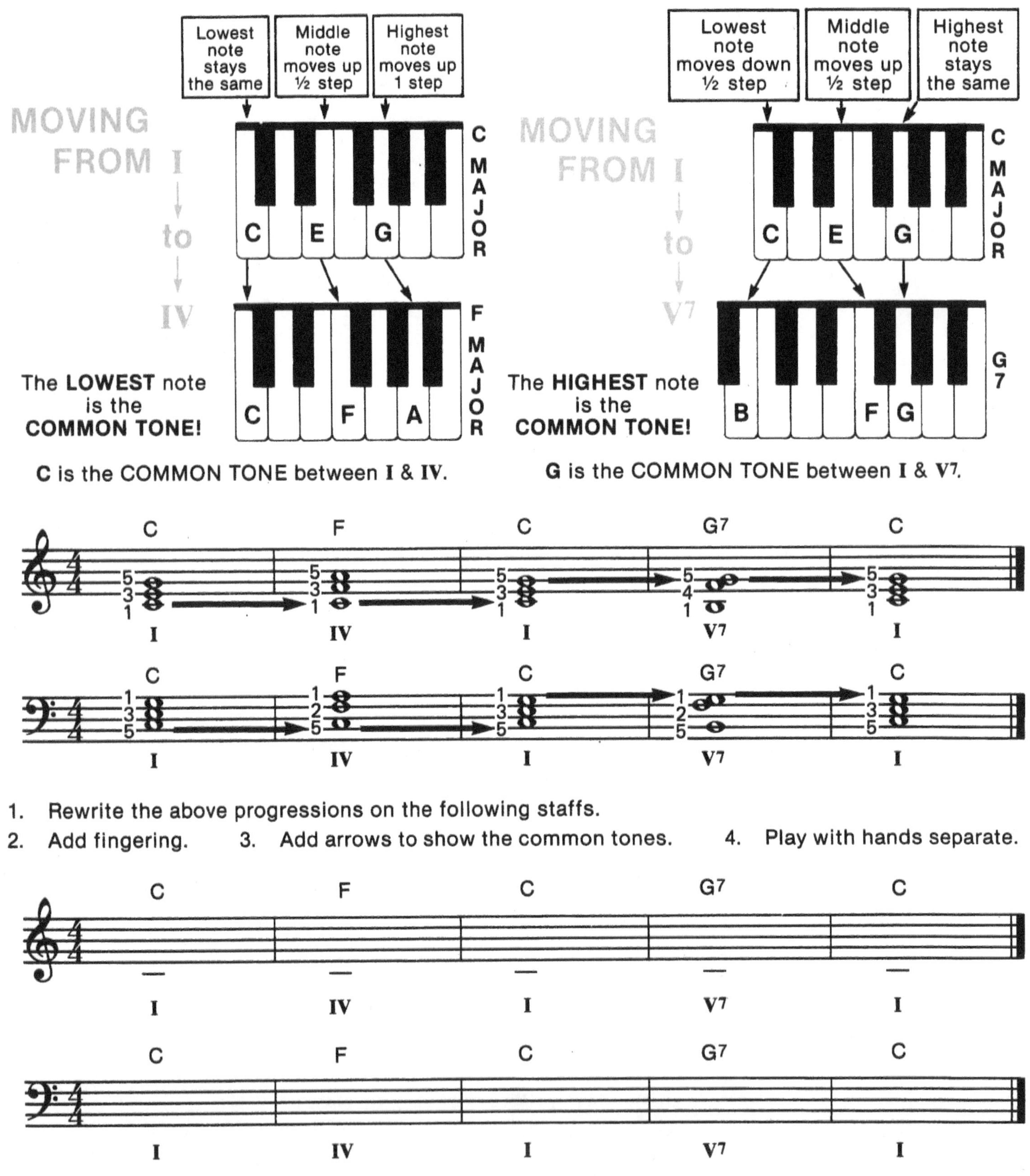

1. Rewrite the above progressions on the following staffs.
2. Add fingering.
3. Add arrows to show the common tones.
4. Play with hands separate.

RH Extended Positions

Assign with pages 4–5.

(Note Reading Review)

Each of the following lines is played with a RH EXTENDED POSITION beginning on a different note.

1. Write the names of the notes in the boxes.
2. Play. Use the damper pedal as indicated.

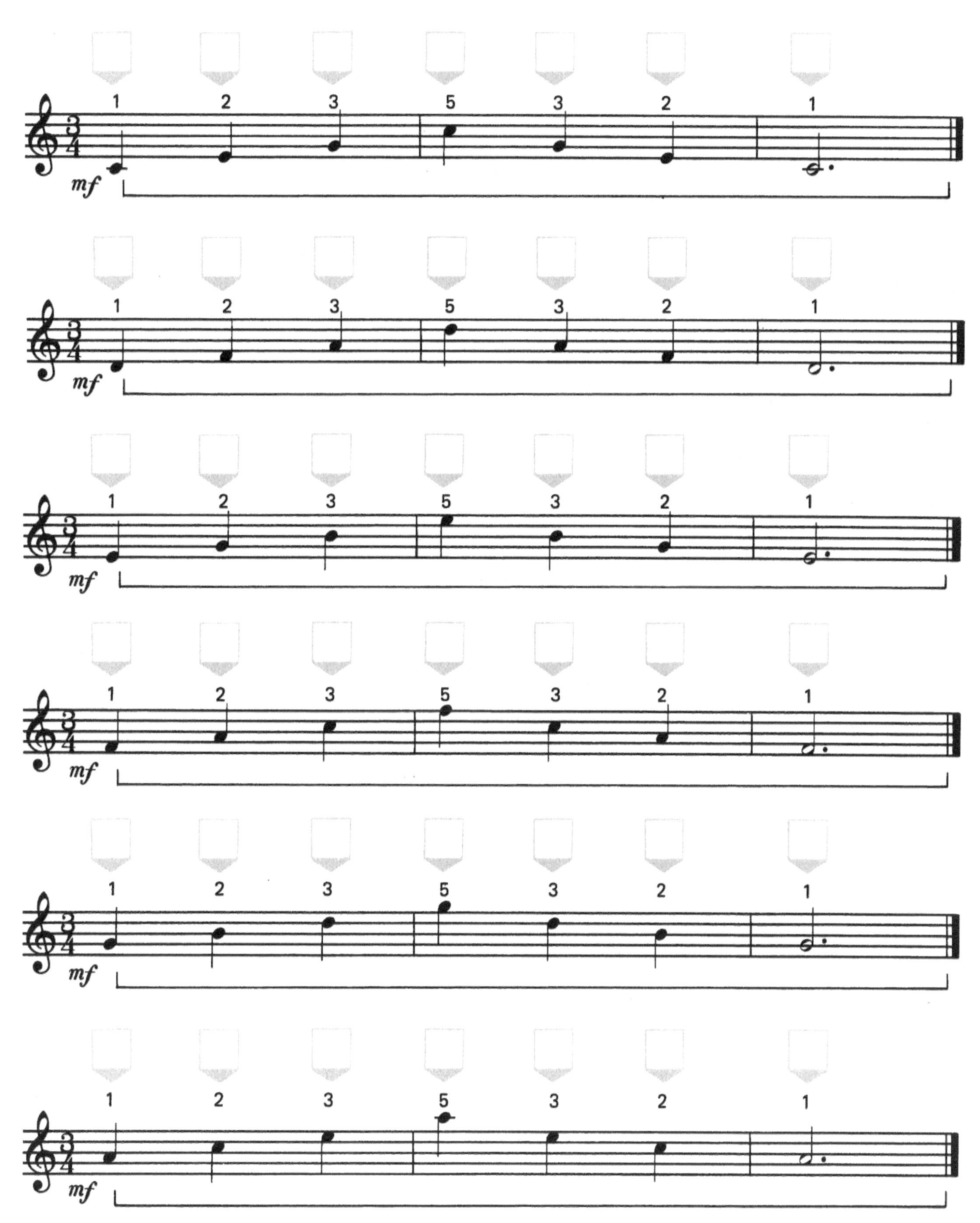

Assign with pages 4–5.

LH Extended Positions

(Note Reading Review)

Each of the following lines is played with a LH EXTENDED POSITION beginning on a different note.

1. Write the names of the notes in the boxes.
2. Play. Use the damper pedal as indicated.

Assign with pages 6-7.

Review—The Key of A Minor

KEY SIGNATURE: NO SHARPS, NO FLATS (relative of C MAJOR).

When you move from the root position of the **i** chord in any MINOR KEY, you also keep the lowest note as a COMMON TONE between **i** & **iv**, and the highest note as a COMMON TONE between **i** and **V7**. You should carefully note how the other tones move.

In the KEY OF A MINOR this works as follows:

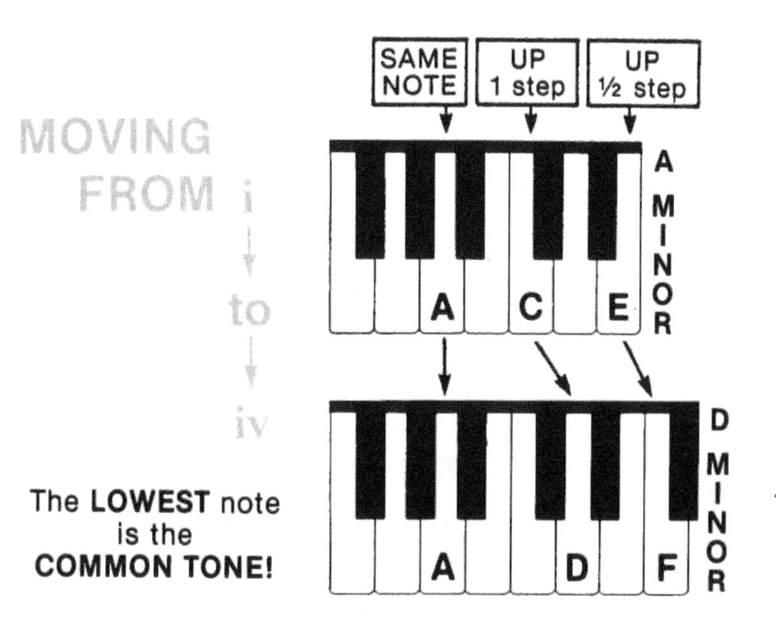

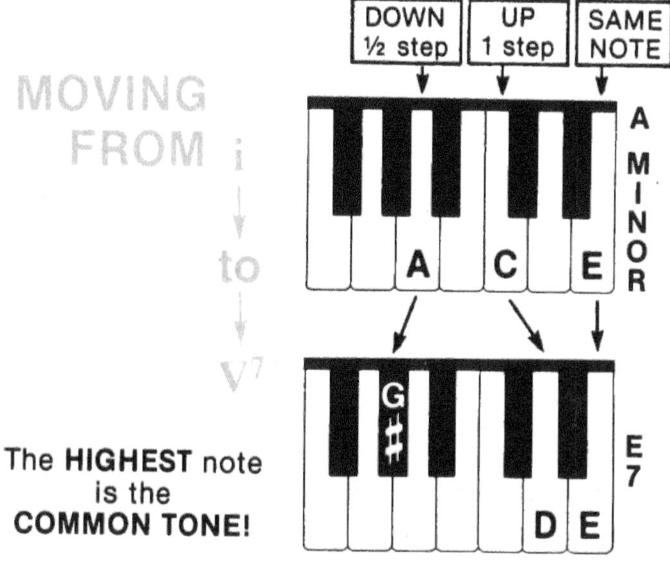

A is the COMMON TONE between **i** & **iv**.

E is the COMMON TONE between **i** & **V7**.

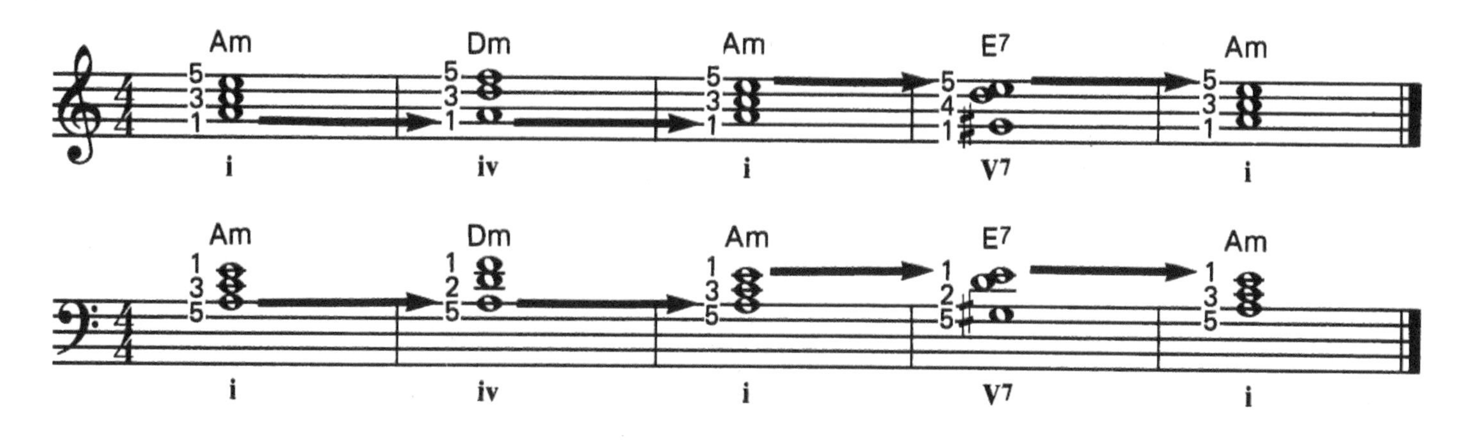

1. Rewrite the above progressions on the following staffs.
2. Add fingering.
3. Add arrows to show the common tones.
4. Play with hands separate.

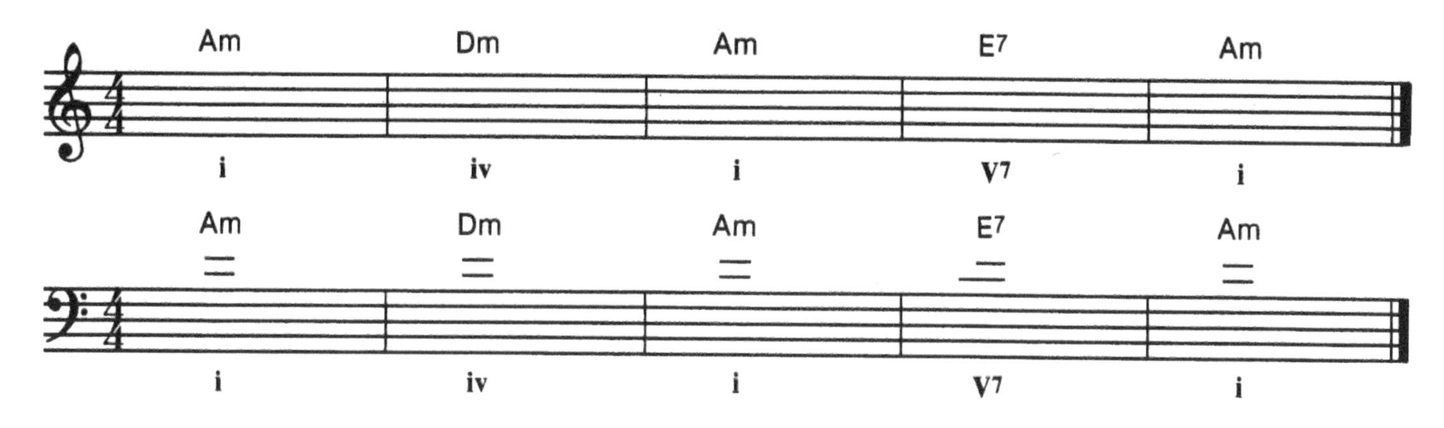

Assign with pages 8-9.

Technique Builder: Crossing 1 Under 2

1. Write the finger numbers OVER each of the following notes, crossing 1 under 2, as shown in the 1st example.
2. Write the names of the notes in the boxes.
3. Play with RH.

4. Write the finger numbers UNDER each of the following notes, crossing 1 under 2, as shown in the 1st example.
5. Write the names of the notes in the boxes.
6. Play with LH.

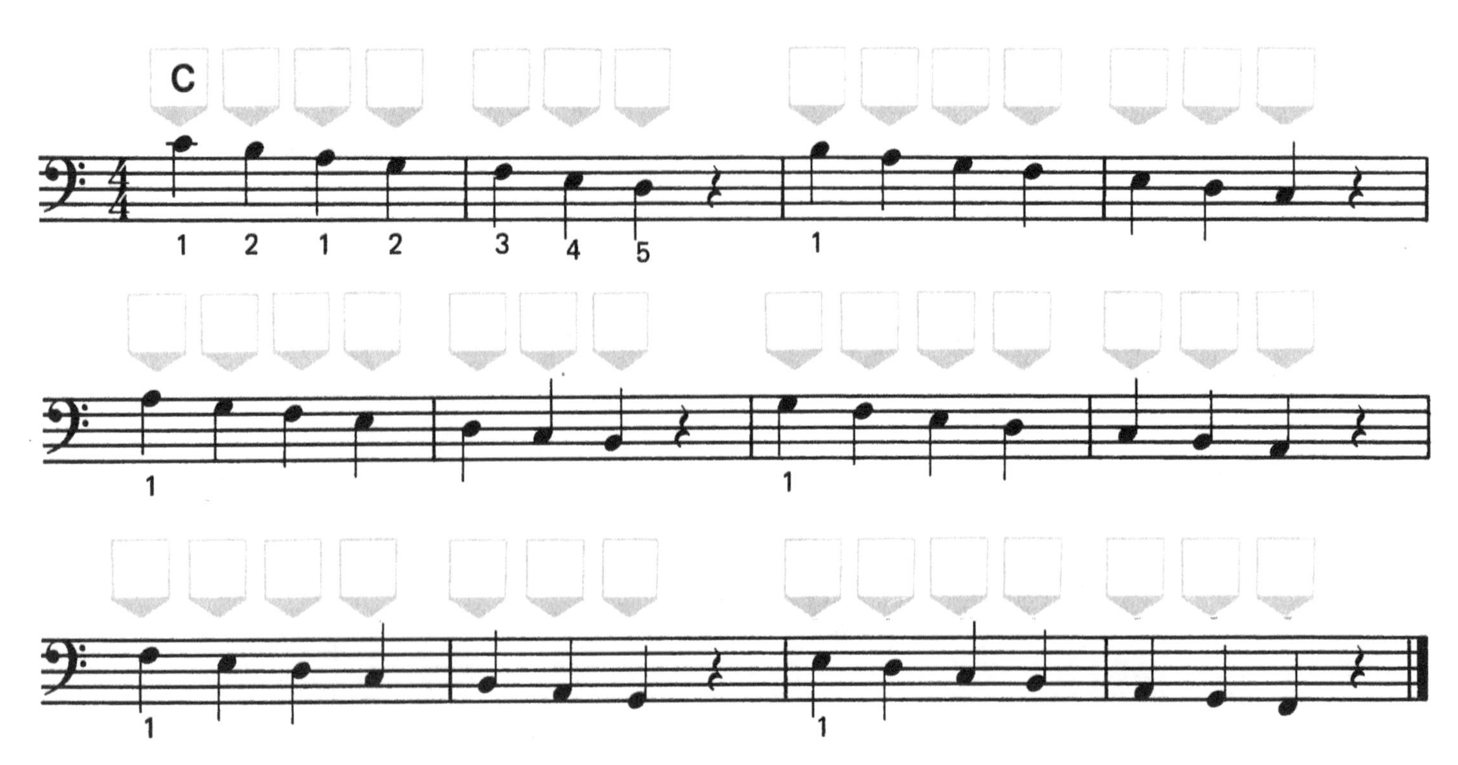

Technique Builder: Crossing 1 Under 3

1. Write the finger numbers OVER each of the following notes, crossing 1 under 3, as shown in the 1st example.
2. Write the names of the notes in the boxes. If a note is sharp, include the sharp in the box.
3. Play with RH.

4. Write the finger numbers UNDER each of the following notes, crossing 1 under 3, as shown in the 1st example.
5. Write the names of the notes in the boxes. Include any sharps that are needed.
6. Play with LH.

Tempo Indications

Assign with pages 12-13.

Tempo means "rate of speed."

The following words are used to tell how fast or slow to play.

Allegro = Quickly, happily

Andante = Moving along ("walking speed")

Moderato = Moderately

Adagio = Slowly

Largo = Very slowly

Moderato may be combined with the other words: **Allegro moderato** = Moderately quick.

1. Select a good tempo for a piece about the following subjects.
2. Write the tempo indication in the box at the beginning of each sentence.

☐	Children running and playing.
☐	A couple strolling on the beach.
☐	A man lazily fishing.
☐	Traffic barely moving during rush hour in a big city.

Review—The Key of F Major

KEY SIGNATURE: ONE FLAT (B♭).

F is the COMMON TONE BETWEEN I & IV. **C** is the COMMON TONE BETWEEN I & V7.

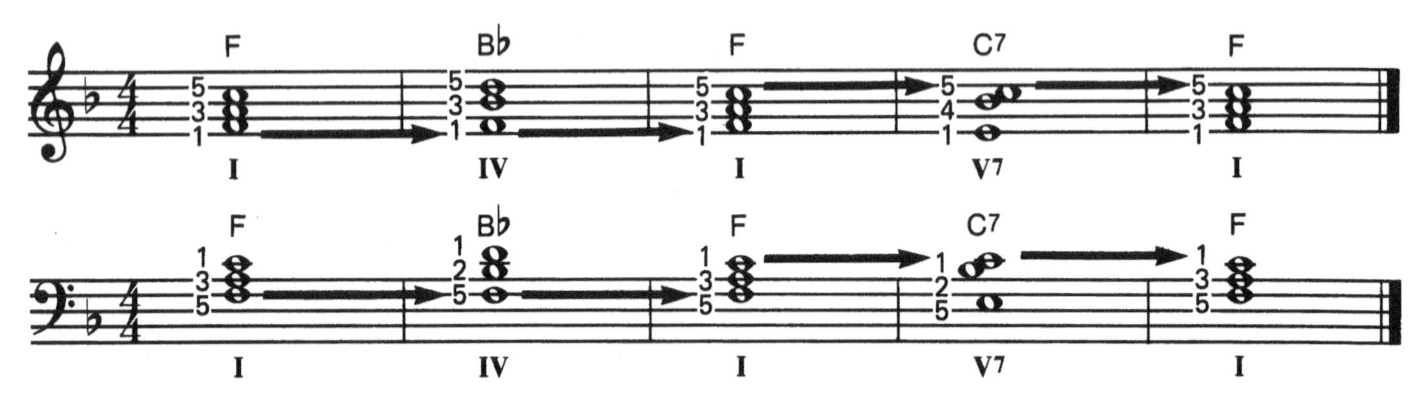

1. Rewrite the above progressions on the following staffs.
2. Add fingering.
3. Add arrows to show the common tones.
4. Play with hands separate.

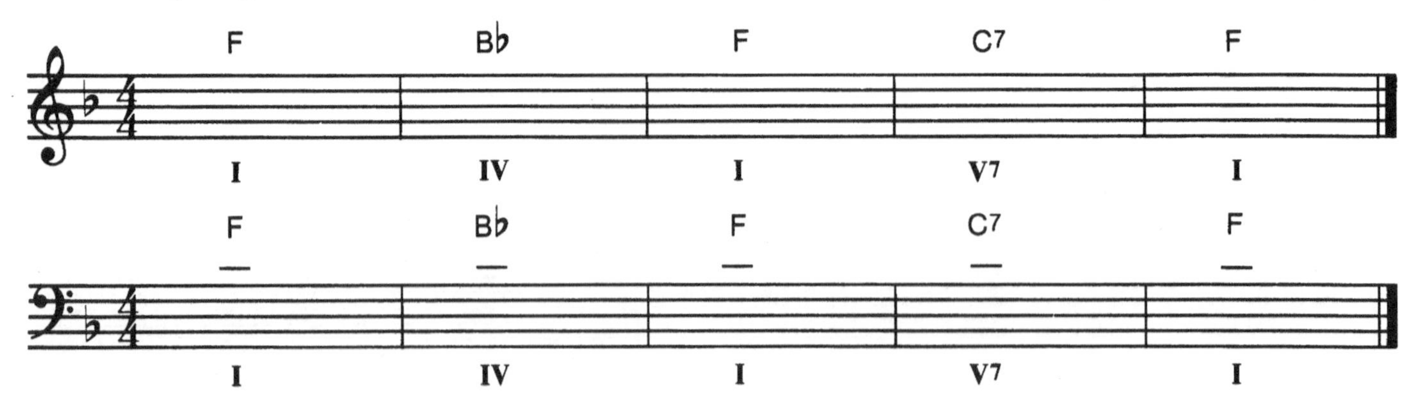

A New Time Signature

Assign with pages 14-15.

means **6** beats to each measure.

means an **eighth note** gets one beat.

In 6/8 time:

1. How many counts does an eighth note get? Answer: ______
2. How many counts does a QUARTER note get? Answer: ______
3. How many counts does a DOTTED QUARTER note get? Answer: ______
4. How many counts does a DOTTED HALF note get? Answer: ______
5. How many counts does this rest (𝄾) get? Answer: ______
6. How many counts does this rest (𝄽) get? Answer: ______
7. How many total counts do these rests (𝄽 𝄾) get? Answer: ______
8. What kind of rest means REST FOR A WHOLE MEASURE? Answer: ______

FOR HE'S A JOLLY GOOD FELLOW

9. Add bar lines. The incomplete measures are completed at the end of each section.
10. Play.

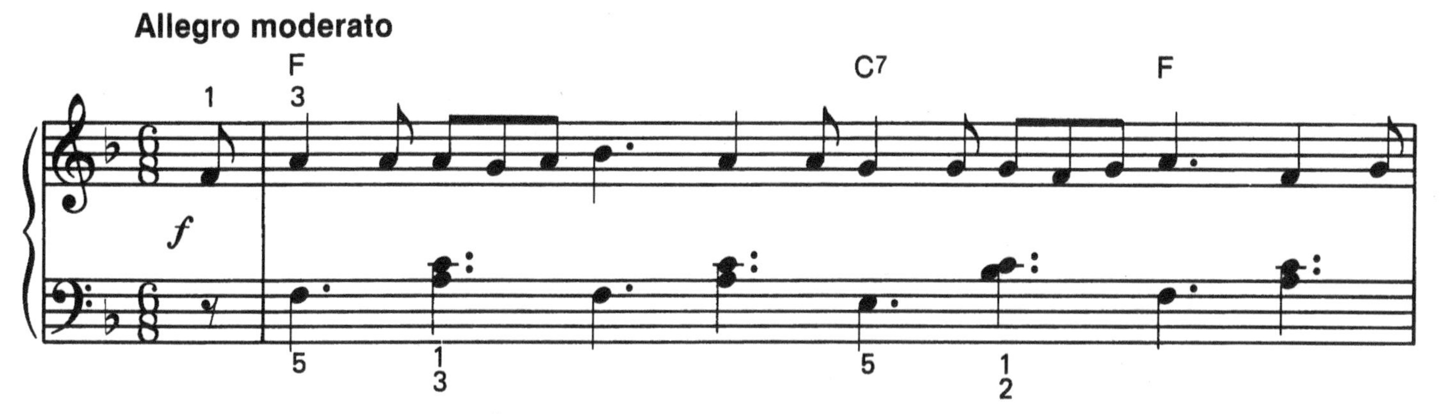

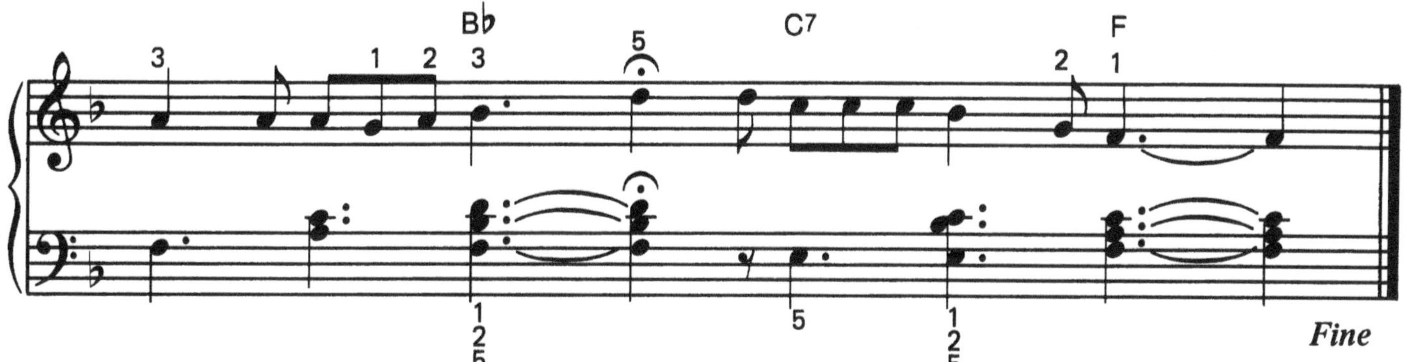

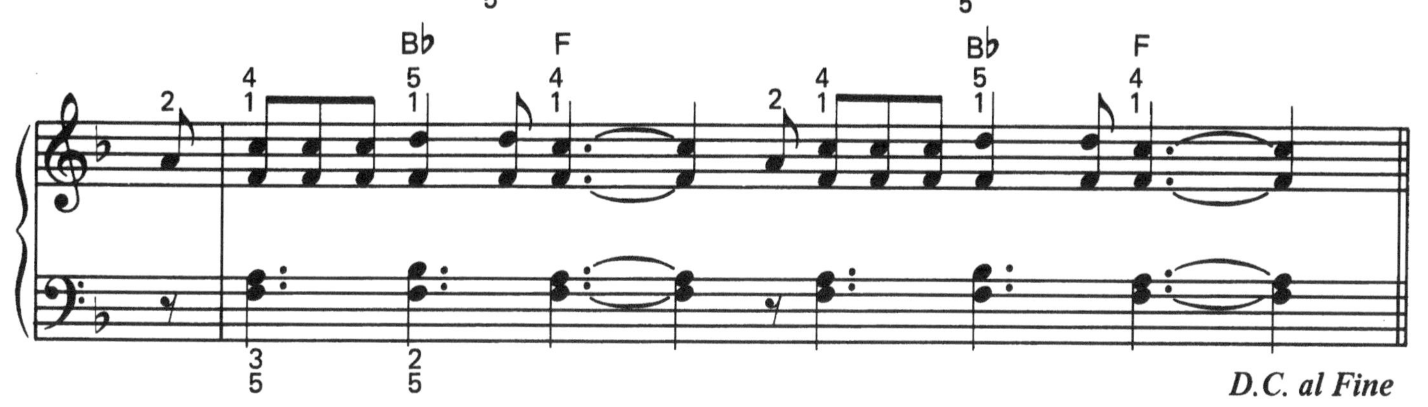

Assign with pages 14–15.

Review—Time Signatures

Each of the following examples represents just ONE MEASURE of music.

1. Write the TIME SIGNATURE at the beginning of each line, as shown in the first example.
2. COUNT ALOUD and TAP (or CLAP) once for each note.

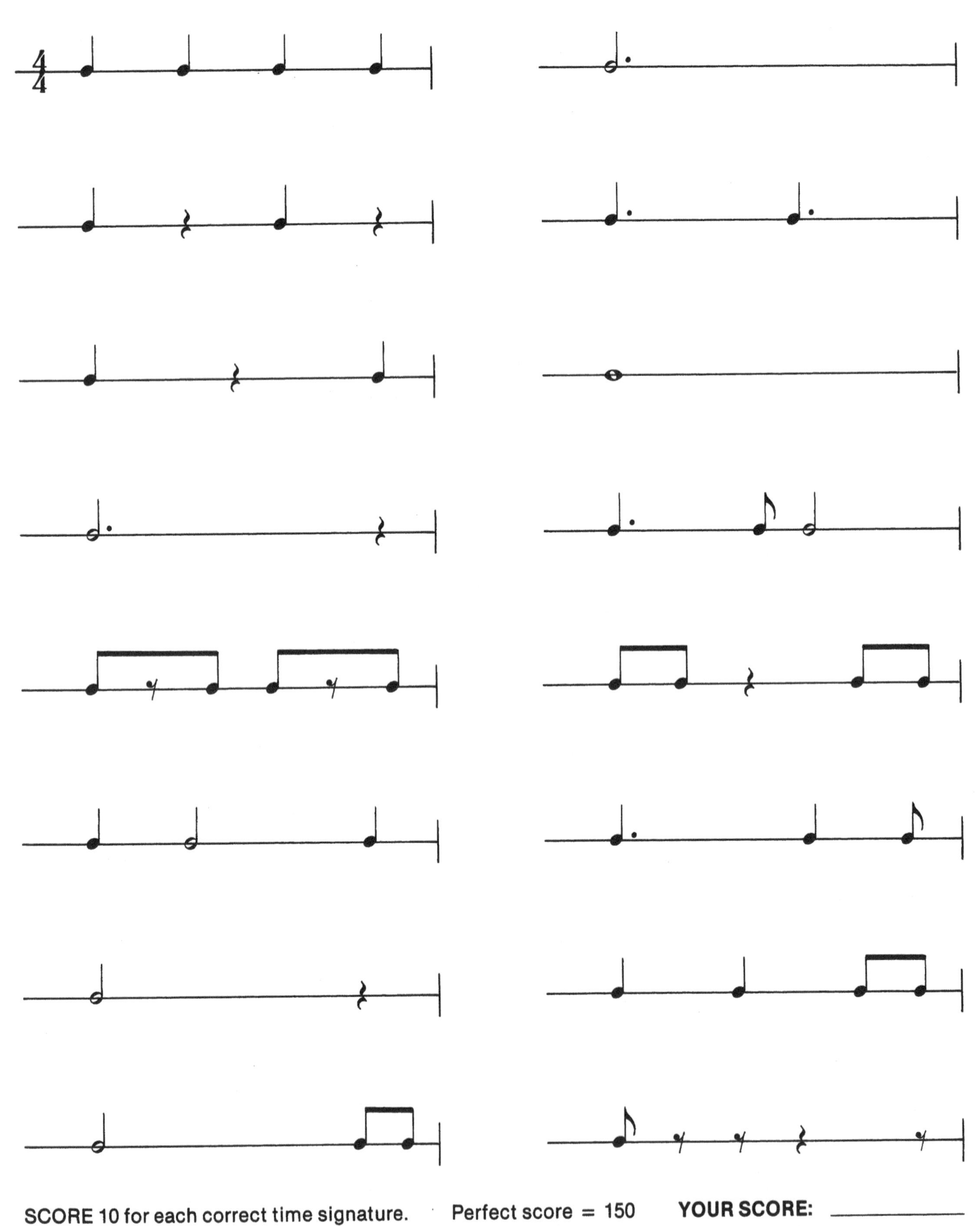

SCORE 10 for each correct time signature. Perfect score = 150 **YOUR SCORE:** __________

Assign with pages 16-19.

Review—The Key of D Minor

KEY SIGNATURE: ONE FLAT (B♭) (relative of F MAJOR).

D is the COMMON TONE BETWEEN **i** & **iv**. **A** is the COMMON TONE between **i** & **V7**.

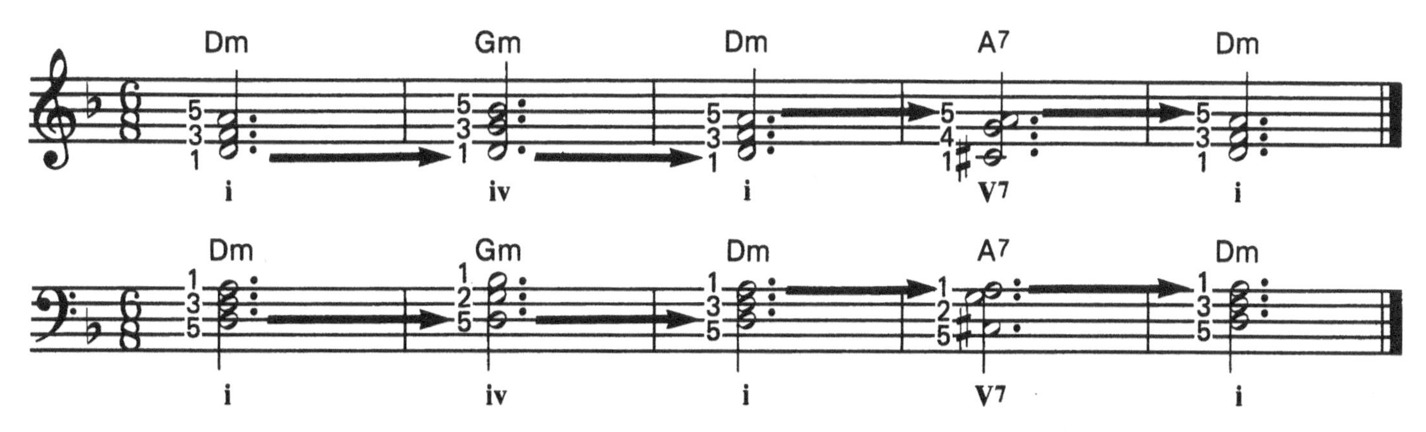

1. Rewrite the above progressions on the following staffs.
2. Add fingering. 3. Add arrows to show the common tones. 4. Play with hands separate.

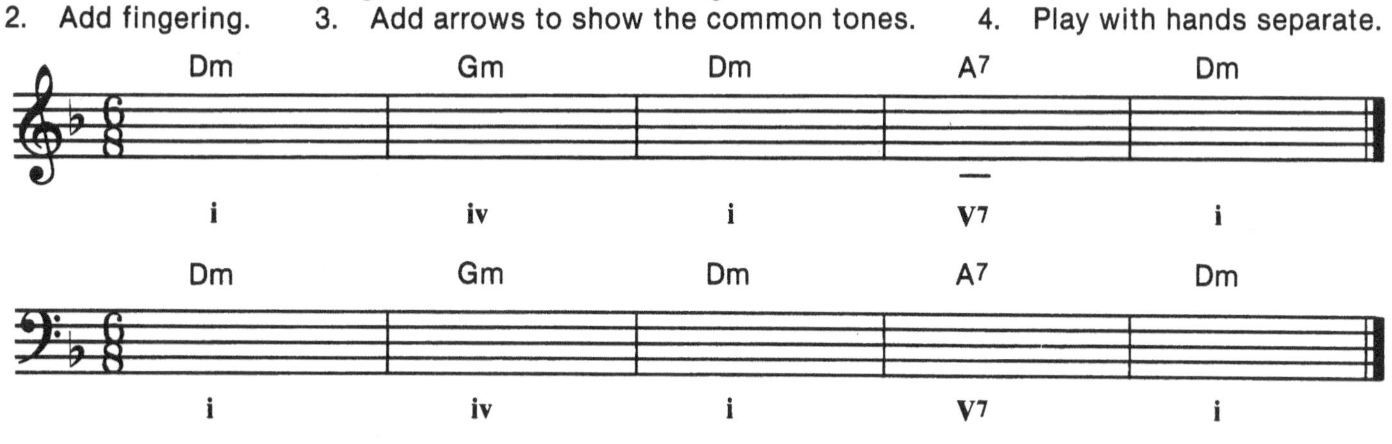

TARANTELLA

5. Add bar lines. The incomplete measure is completed at the end.
6. Play.

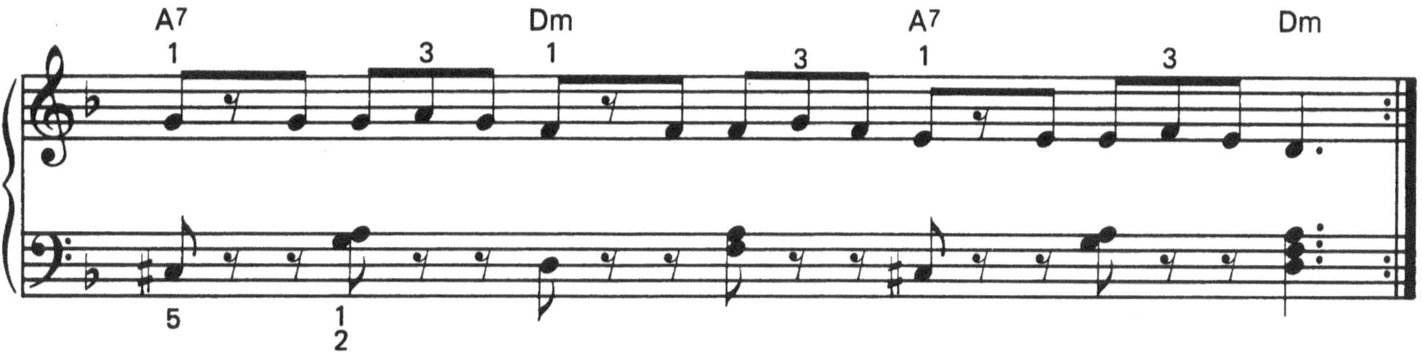

Assign with pages 20-21.

Review—The Key of G Major

KEY SIGNATURE: ONE SHARP (F♯)

G is the COMMON TONE between **I** & **IV**. **D** is the common tone between **I** & **V7**.

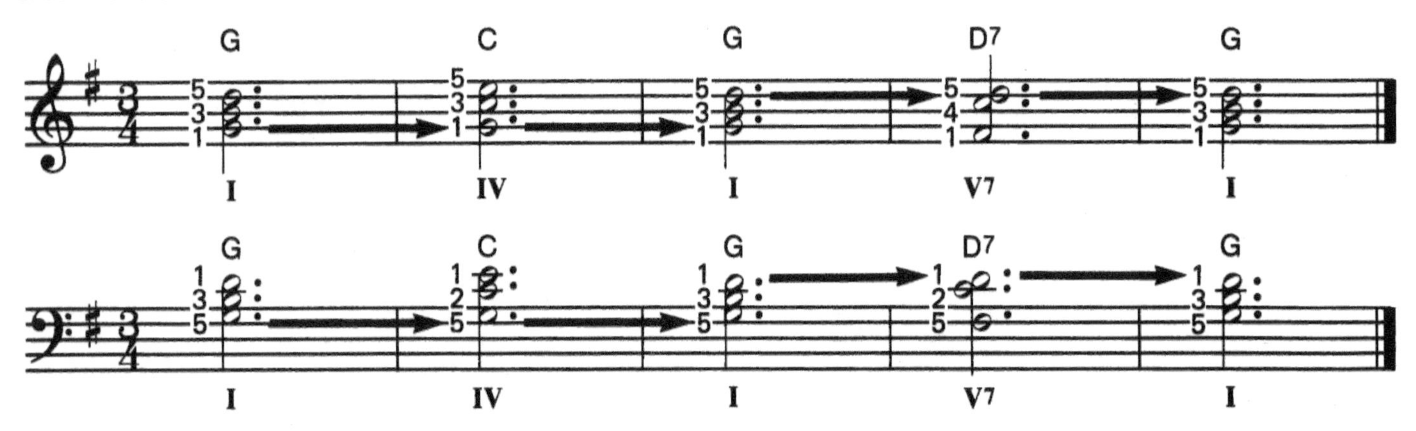

1. Rewrite the above progressions on the following staffs.
2. Add fingering.
3. Add arrows to show the common tones.
4. Play with hands separate.

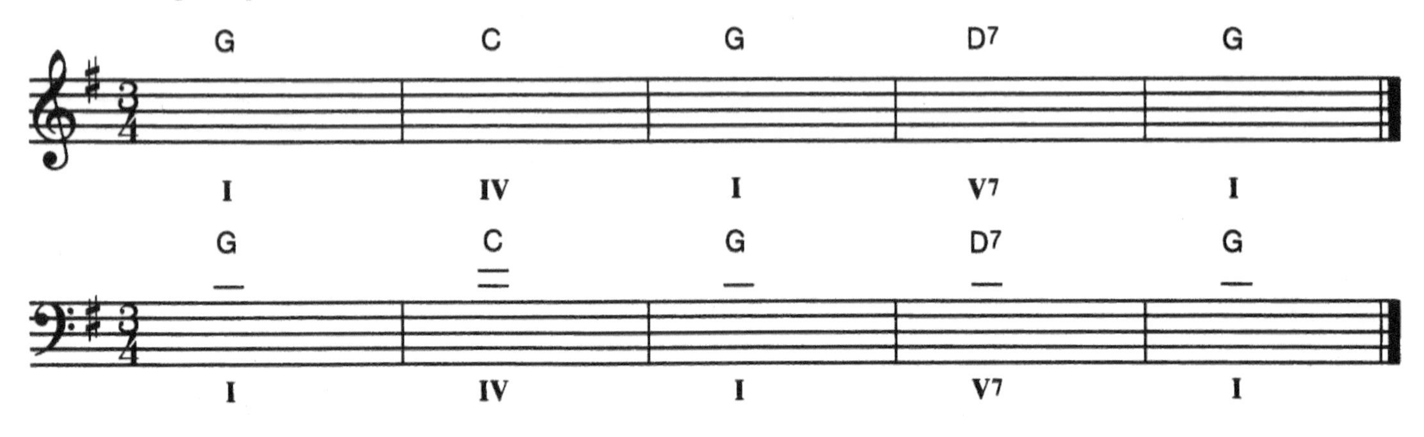

More About Extended Positions

EXTENDED POSITIONS often skip a 3rd between the 1st and 2nd fingers, and a 4th between the 2nd and 3rd fingers. Sometimes they skip a 4th between the 1st and 2nd, and a 3rd between the 2nd and 3rd.

1. Write the names of the notes in the boxes.
2. Play, carefully observing the intervals between the notes.

Assign with pages 22-23.

The Key of E Minor (Relative of G Major)

E MINOR is the relative of **G MAJOR.**
Both keys have the same key signature (1 sharp, F♯).
REMEMBER: The RELATIVE MINOR begins on the 6th tone of the MAJOR SCALE.

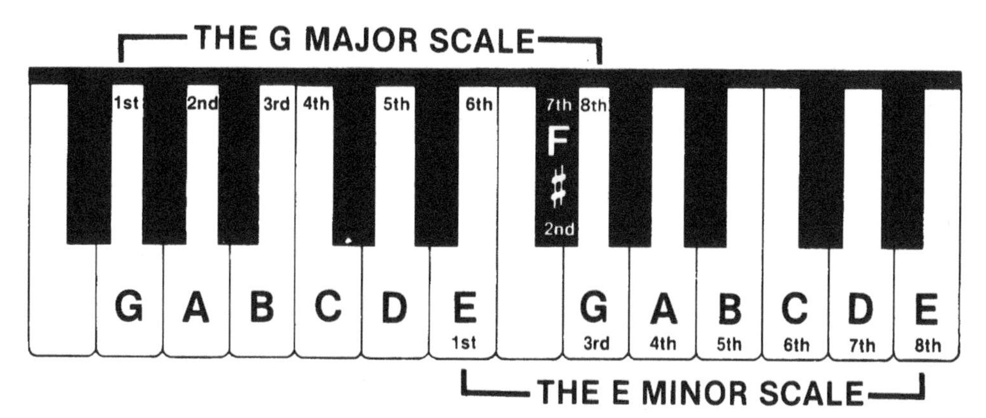

THE NATURAL MINOR SCALE. This scale uses *only* the tones of the relative major scale.

1. Play with hands separate.

KEY OF E MINOR
Key Signature: 1 sharp (F♯)

THE HARMONIC MINOR SCALE. The 7th tone (D) is raised 1 half step, ASCENDING & DESCENDING.

2. Add accidentals needed to change these NATURAL MINOR scales into HARMONIC MINOR scales.
3. Play with hands separate.

THE MELODIC MINOR SCALE. 6th (C) and 7th (D) raised 1 half step ASCENDING; descends like natural minor.

4. Add accidentals needed to change these NATURAL MINOR scales into MELODIC MINOR scales.
5. Play with hands separate.

6. (Optional) Play all of the above scales with hands together.

Assign with pages 24-27.

The Primary Chords in E Minor

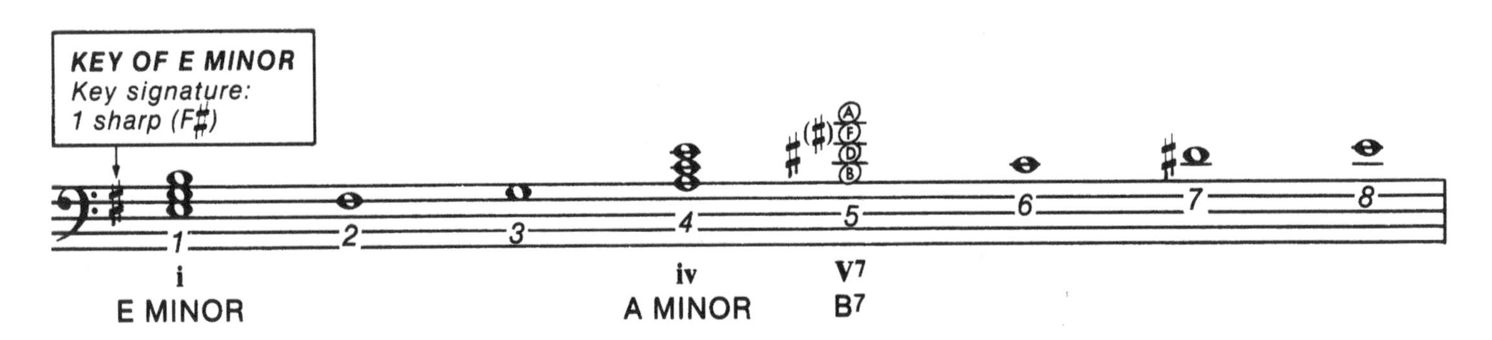

These positions are used for smooth progressions:

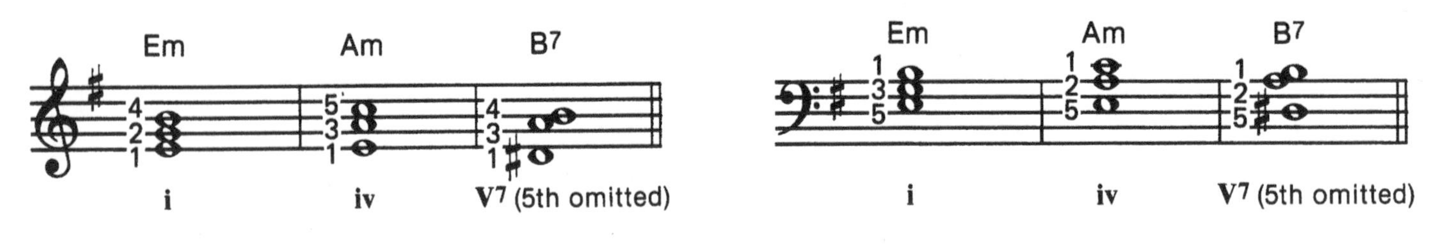

E is the COMMON TONE between **i** & **iv**. **B** is the COMMON TONE between **i** & **V7**.

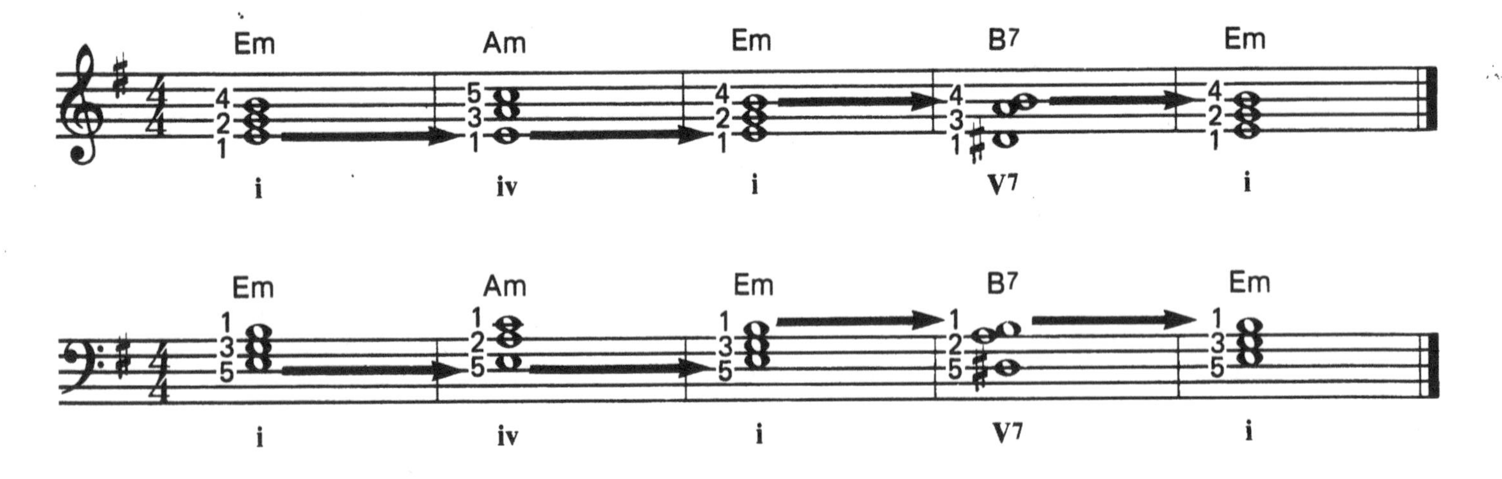

1. Rewrite the above progressions on the following staffs.
2. Add fingering.
3. Add arrows to show the common tones.
4. Play with hands separate.

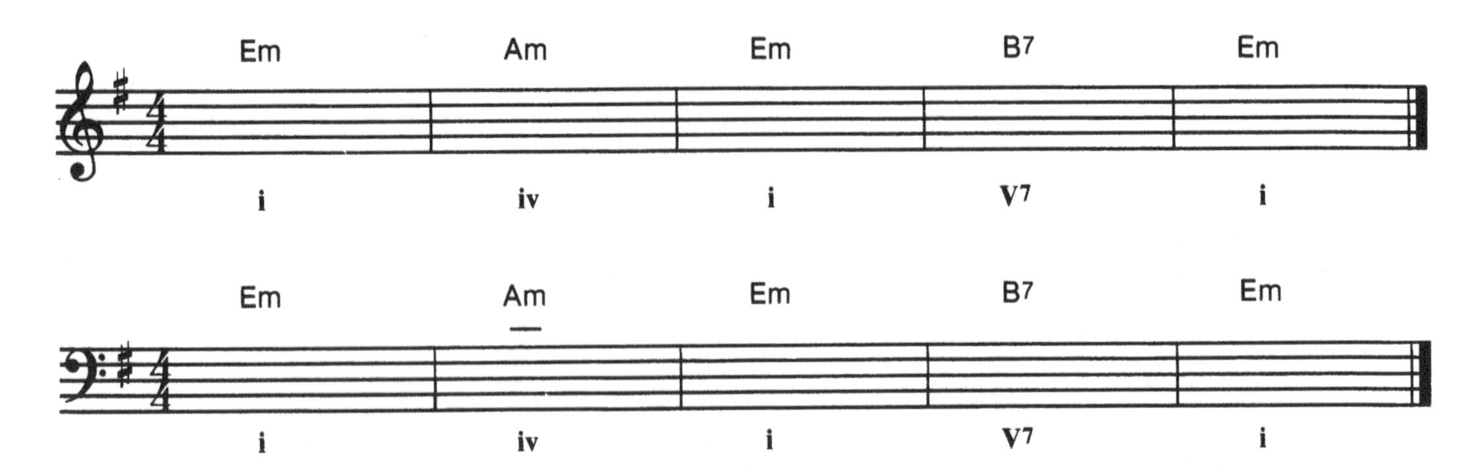

Assign with pages 28-29.

The Key of D Major

1. Write the letter names of the notes of the D MAJOR SCALE, from *left to right,* on the keyboard below. Be sure the WHOLE STEPS & HALF STEPS are correct!

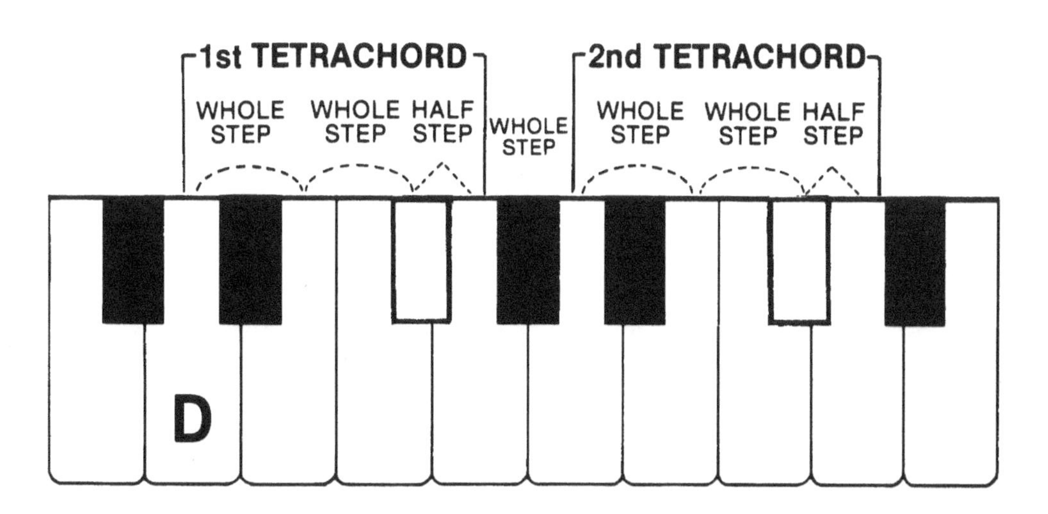

2. Check to be sure you wrote F♯ as the 3rd note of the scale, and C♯ as the 7th note. These notes cannot be called G♭ and D♭, since scale note names must always be in alphabetical order.

3. Complete the tetrachord beginning on D. Write one note over each finger number.

4. Complete the tetrachord beginning on A. Write one note over each finger number.

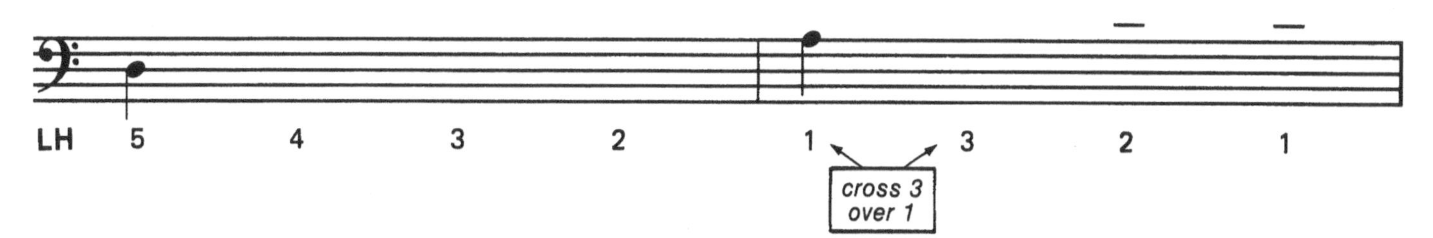

5. Write the fingering UNDER each note of the following LH scale.
6. Play with LH.

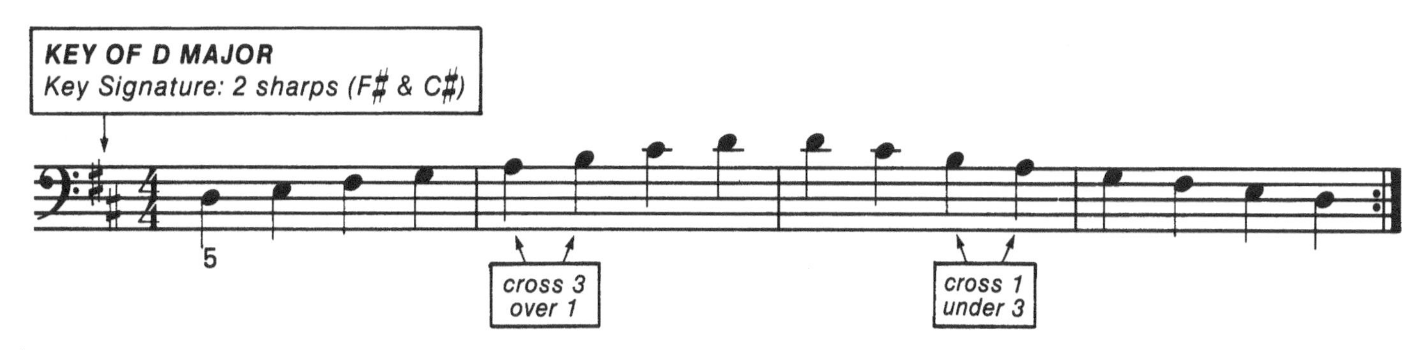

7. Write the fingering OVER each note of the following RH scale.
8. Play with RH.

Assign with pages 30–33.

Primary Chords in D Major

KEY OF D MAJOR
Key Signature:
two sharps (F♯ and C♯)

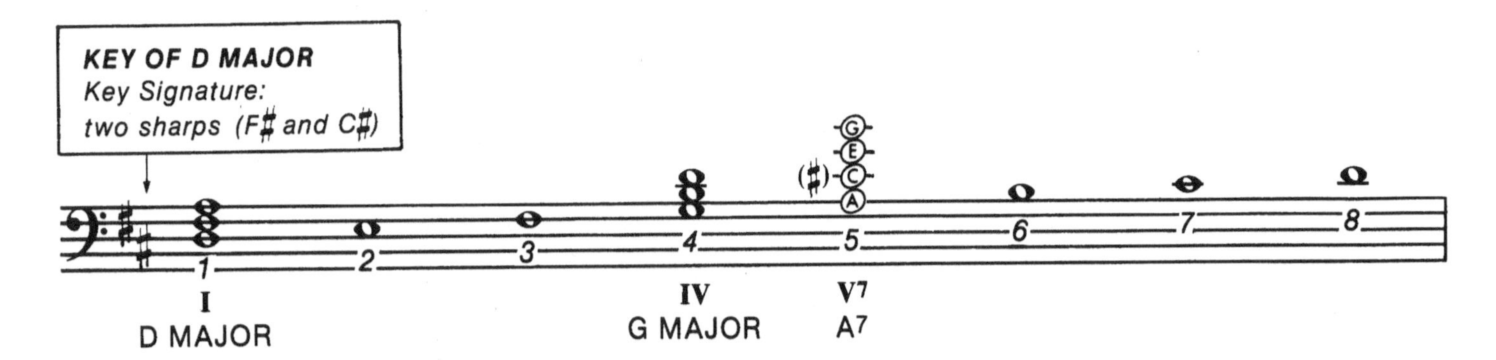

The following positions are often used for smooth progressions:

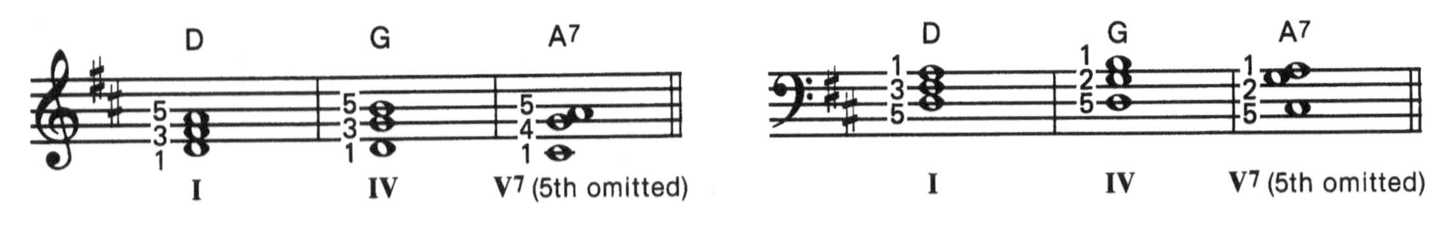

D is the COMMON TONE between **I & IV**. **A** is the COMMON TONE between **I & V7**.

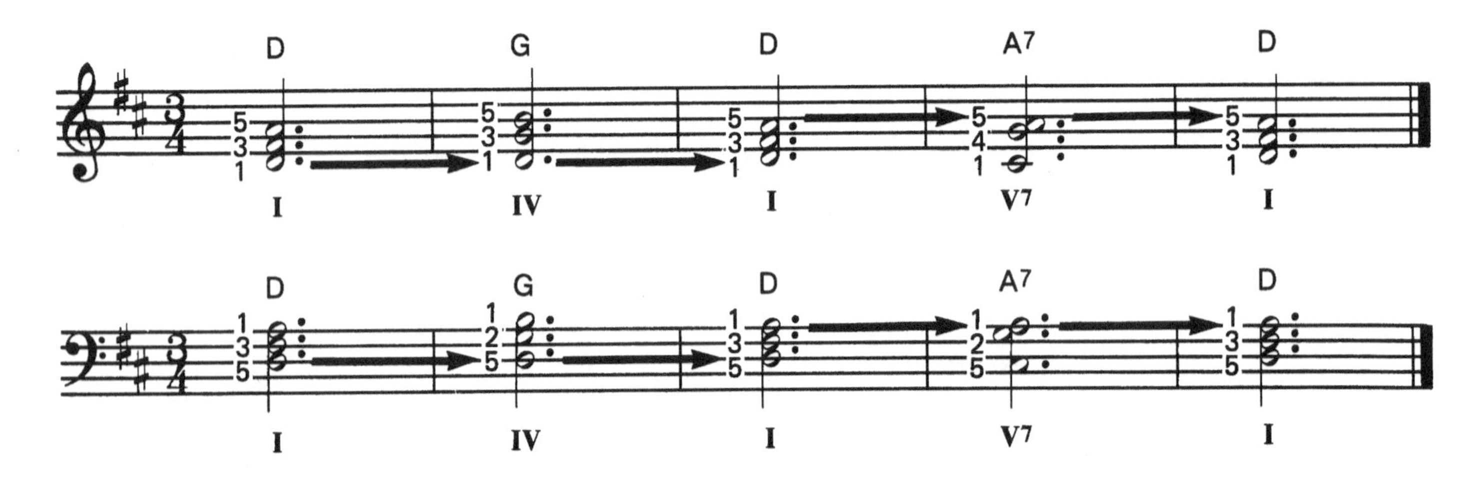

1. Rewrite the above progressions on the following staffs.
2. Add fingering.
3. Add arrows to show the common tones.
4. Play with hands separate.

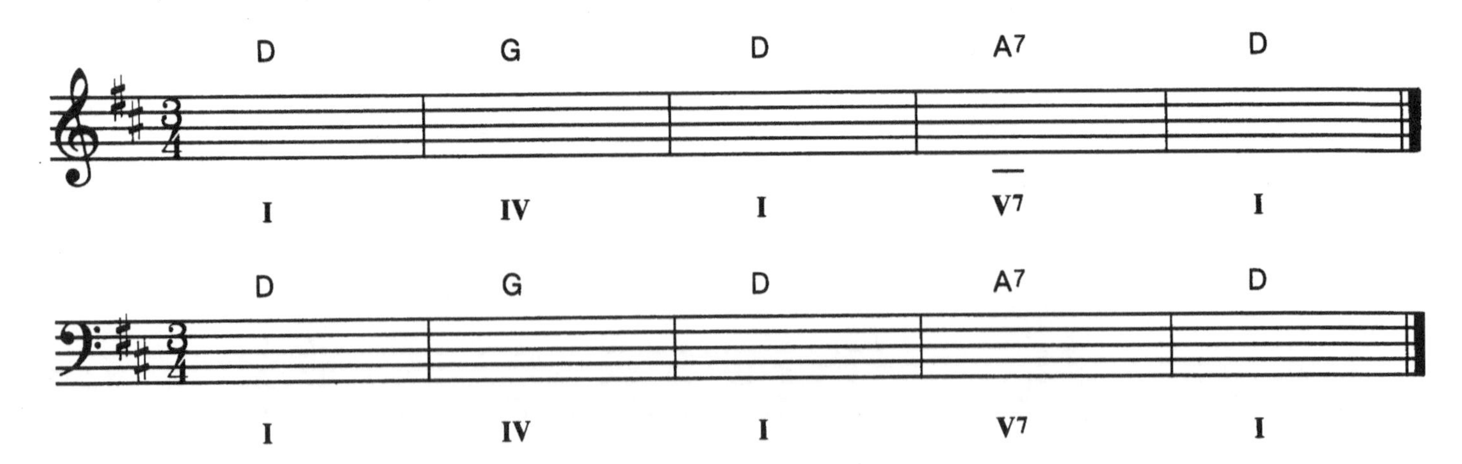

Assign with pages 34-35.

The Chromatic Scale

The **CHROMATIC SCALE** is made up entirely of **HALF STEPS.**
It goes up and down, using every key, black and white. It may begin on any note.

FINGERING RULES

- Use 3 on each BLACK KEY.
- Use 1 on each white key, except when two white keys are together (no black key between), then use 1-2, or 2-1.

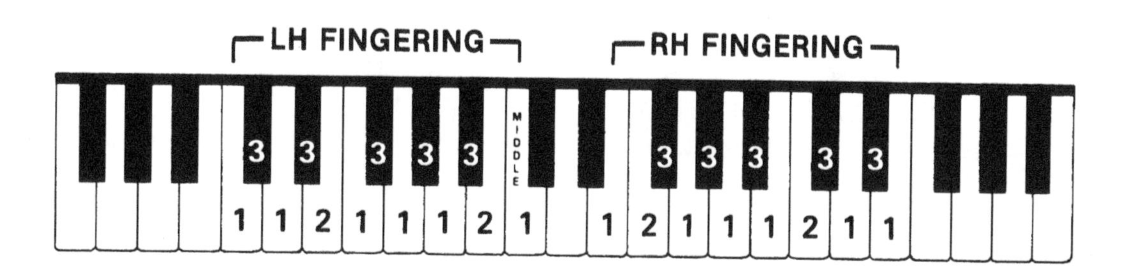

1. Write the chromatic scale, ASCENDING, on the following TREBLE STAFF. (Use half notes.) Use SHARPS to indicate BLACK KEYS.
2. Write the chromatic scale, DESCENDING, on the BASS STAFF. Use FLATS to indicate BLACK KEYS.

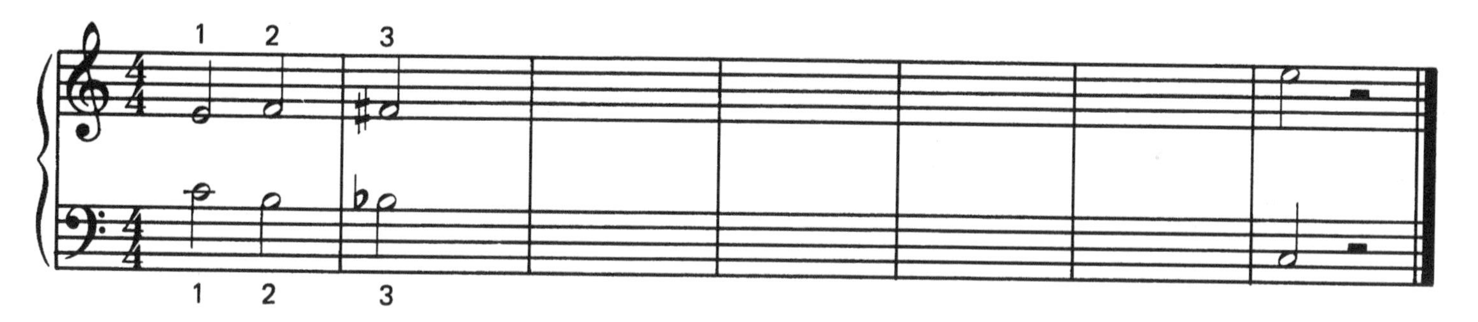

3. Write the chromatic scale DESCENDING, on the following TREBLE STAFF. Use FLATS to indicate BLACK KEYS.
4. Write the chromatic scale, ASCENDING, on the BASS STAFF. Use SHARPS to indicate BLACK KEYS.

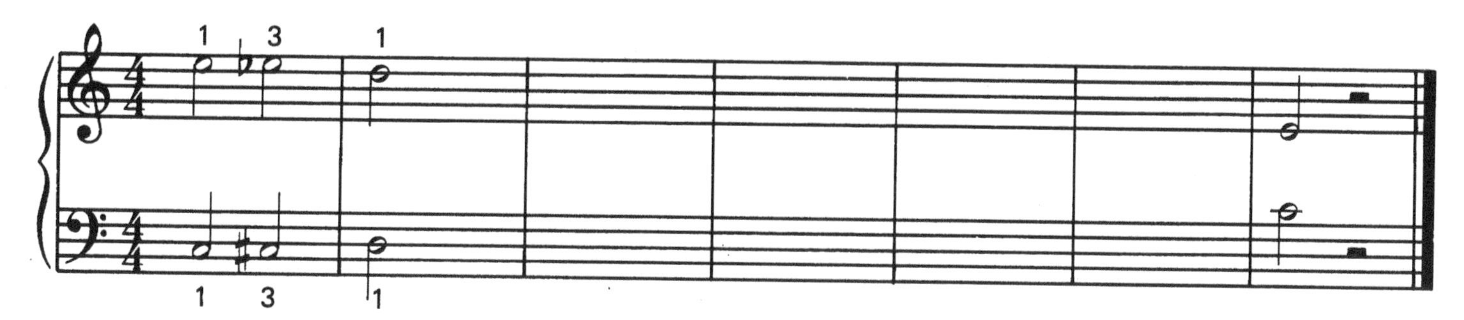

5. Add fingering to the above measures, using the FINGERING RULES at the top of this page.
6. Play everything on this page, hands separately.

   You may also play with hands together, if you wish. When you begin with RH on E and LH on C and play in contrary motion, as you have written above, both hands will use the same fingers at the same time. The chromatic scale is very easy to play in contrary motion.

Assign with pages 36–39.

TRIADS: The 1st Inversion

ANY ROOT POSITION TRIAD MAY BE INVERTED BY MOVING THE ROOT TO THE TOP.

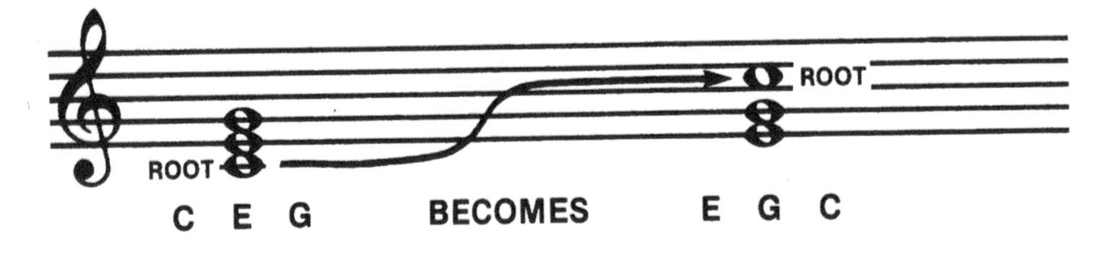

LETTER NAMES ARE THE SAME, BUT THE ROOT IS ON TOP.
THE 3rd OF THE TRIAD IS NOW ON THE BOTTOM!
This is called the 1st INVERSION.

1. In the measure following each ROOT POSITION triad, write the same triad in the 1st INVERSION.

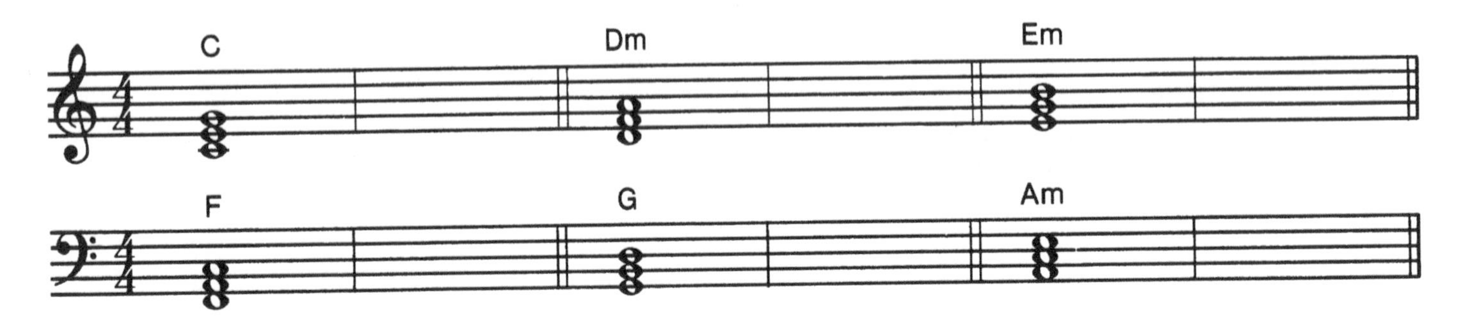

2. Play the TOP LINE above with the RH. Use 1 3 5 on the ROOT POSITION triads. Use 1 2 5 on the 1st INVERSION triads.
3. Play the BOTTOM LINE above with the LH. Use 5 3 1 on the ROOT POSITION triads. Use 5 3 1 also on the 1st INVERSION triads.

Triads in the 1st INVERSION look like this: When a triad has this appearance, the note at the TOP of the interval of a 4th is the ROOT!

4. Draw an arrow (←) pointing to the ROOT of each triad in No. 1, above.

CHORALE

5. Using the notes given below as ROOTS, add 2 notes below each to make 1st INVERSION triads.
6. Play. Use RH 1 2 5 on the notes in treble clef. Use LH 5 3 1 on the notes in bass clef.

Assign with pages 36-39.

Invert the Triads!

Each triad in the left column is in ROOT POSITION.

1. Write the letter names on each keyboard in the right column, showing the same triad in the 1st INVERSION.
2. Draw arrows pointing UP to the ROOT of *each* root position and 1st inversion triad. The first pair of triads is completed for you, as an example.

ROOT POSITION

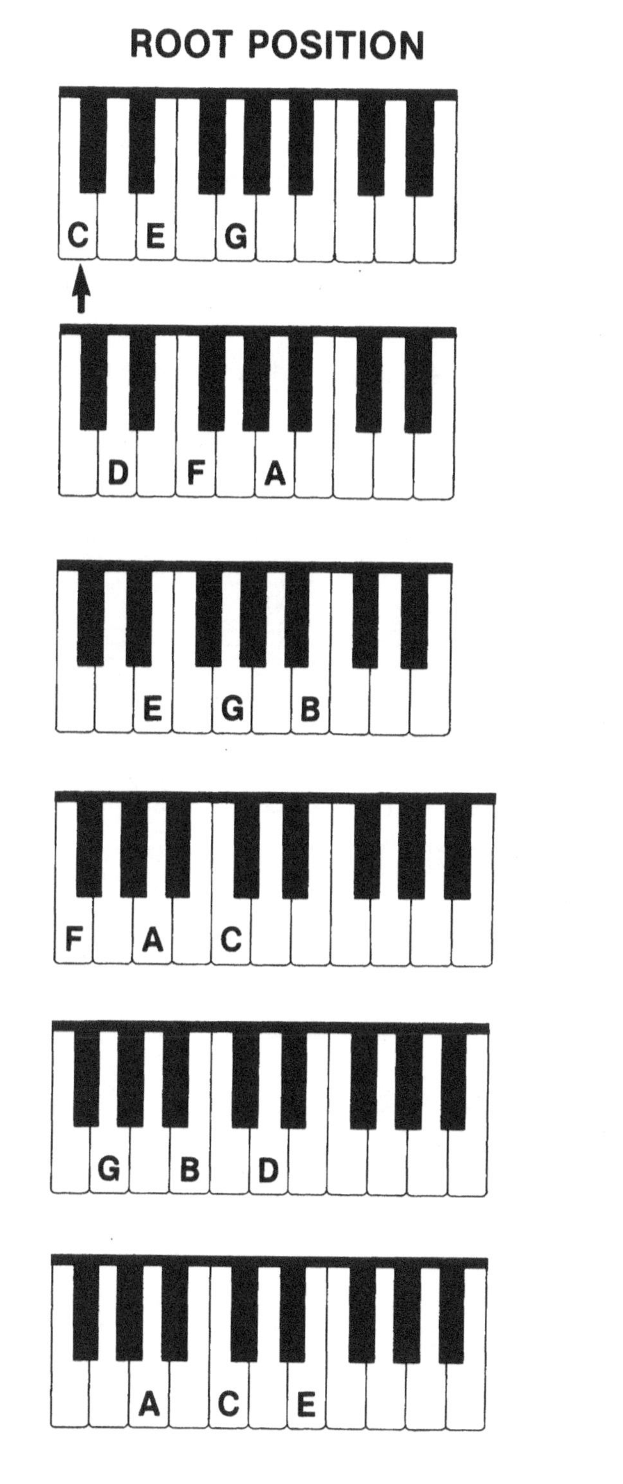

1st INVERSION

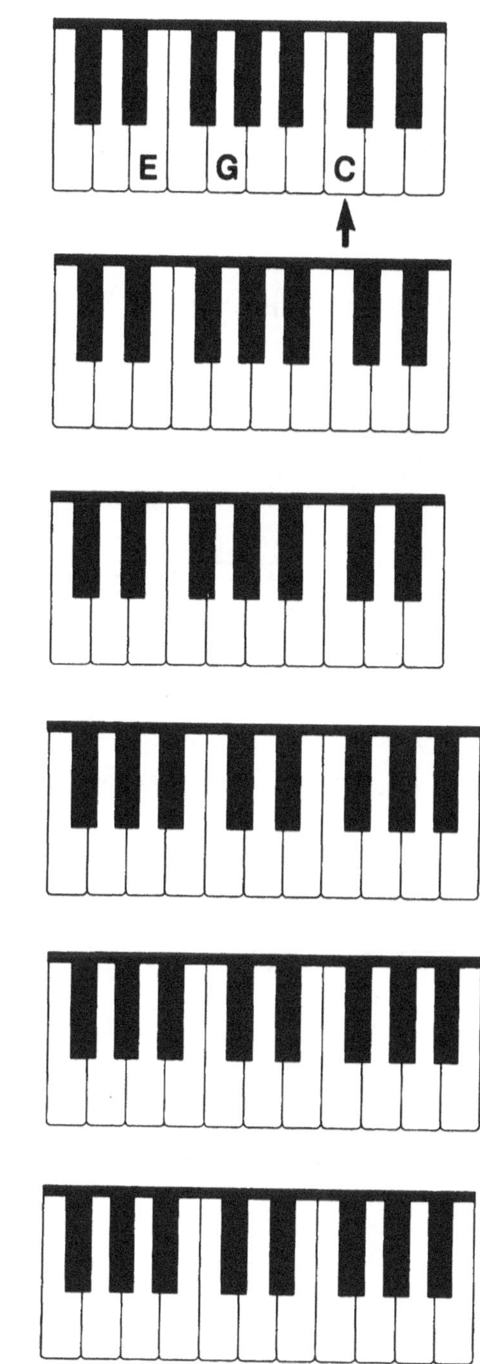

3. BONUS QUESTION: When a triad is in the 1st INVERSION, which note is on the BOTTOM?

ANSWER: ROOT THIRD FIFTH (Circle the right answer.)

Score 10 for each correct 1st INVERSION TRIAD. ________
Score 2 for each correct ARROW. ________
Score 30 for BONUS QUESTION. ________
PERFECT SCORE = 100. YOUR SCORE: ________

TRIADS: The 2nd Inversion

Assign with pages 40–41.

ANY 1st INVERSION TRIAD MAY BE INVERTED AGAIN BY MOVING THE LOWEST NOTE TO THE TOP.

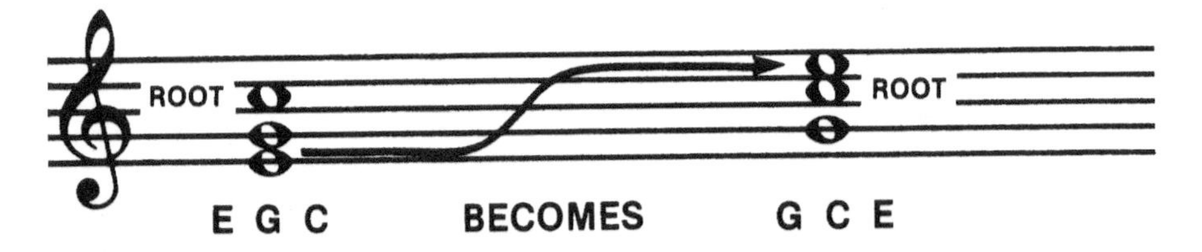

LETTER NAMES ARE THE SAME, BUT THE ROOT IS IN THE MIDDLE.
THE 5th OF THE TRIAD IS NOW ON THE BOTTOM!
This is called the 2nd INVERSION.

1. In the measure following each 1st inversion triad, write the same triad in the 2nd INVERSION.

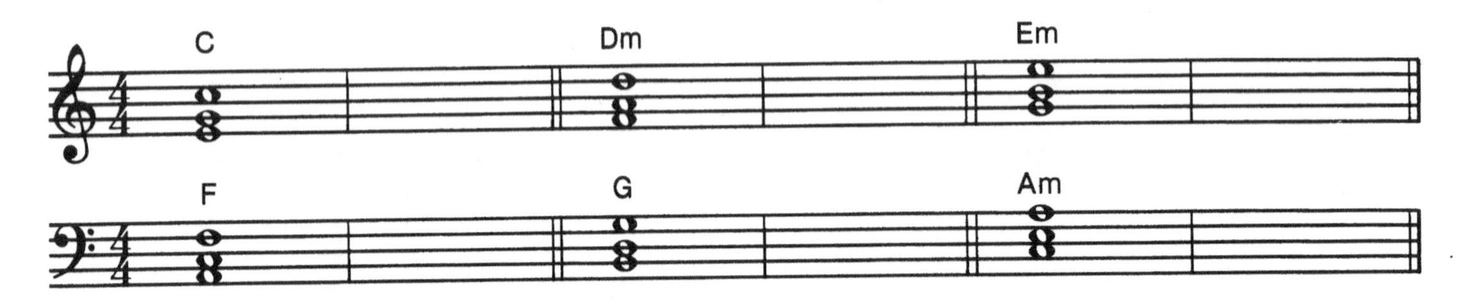

2. Play the TOP LINE above with the RH. Use 1 2 5 on the 1st INVERSION triads.
3. Play the BOTTOM LINE above with the LH. Use 5 3 1 on the 1st INVERSION triads. Use 5 2 1 on the 2nd INVERSION triads.

Triads in the 2nd INVERSION look like this: When a triad has this appearance, the note at the TOP of the interval of a 4th is the ROOT!

4. Draw an arrow (⟵) pointing to the ROOT of each triad in No. 1, above.

CHORALE

5. Using the notes given in the TREBLE CLEF above as ROOTS, add a note above and a note below each to make 2nd INVERSION TRIADS. (Add notes only in the UPPER STAFF.)
6. Play. Use 1 3 5 on each RH triad.

Assign with pages 40-41.

Invert the Inversions!

Each triad in the left column is in the 1st INVERSION.

1. Write the letter names on each keyboard in the right column, showing the same triad in the 2nd INVERSION.
2. Draw arrows pointing UP to the ROOT of *each* 1st and 2nd INVERSION triad. The first pair of triads is completed for you, as an example.

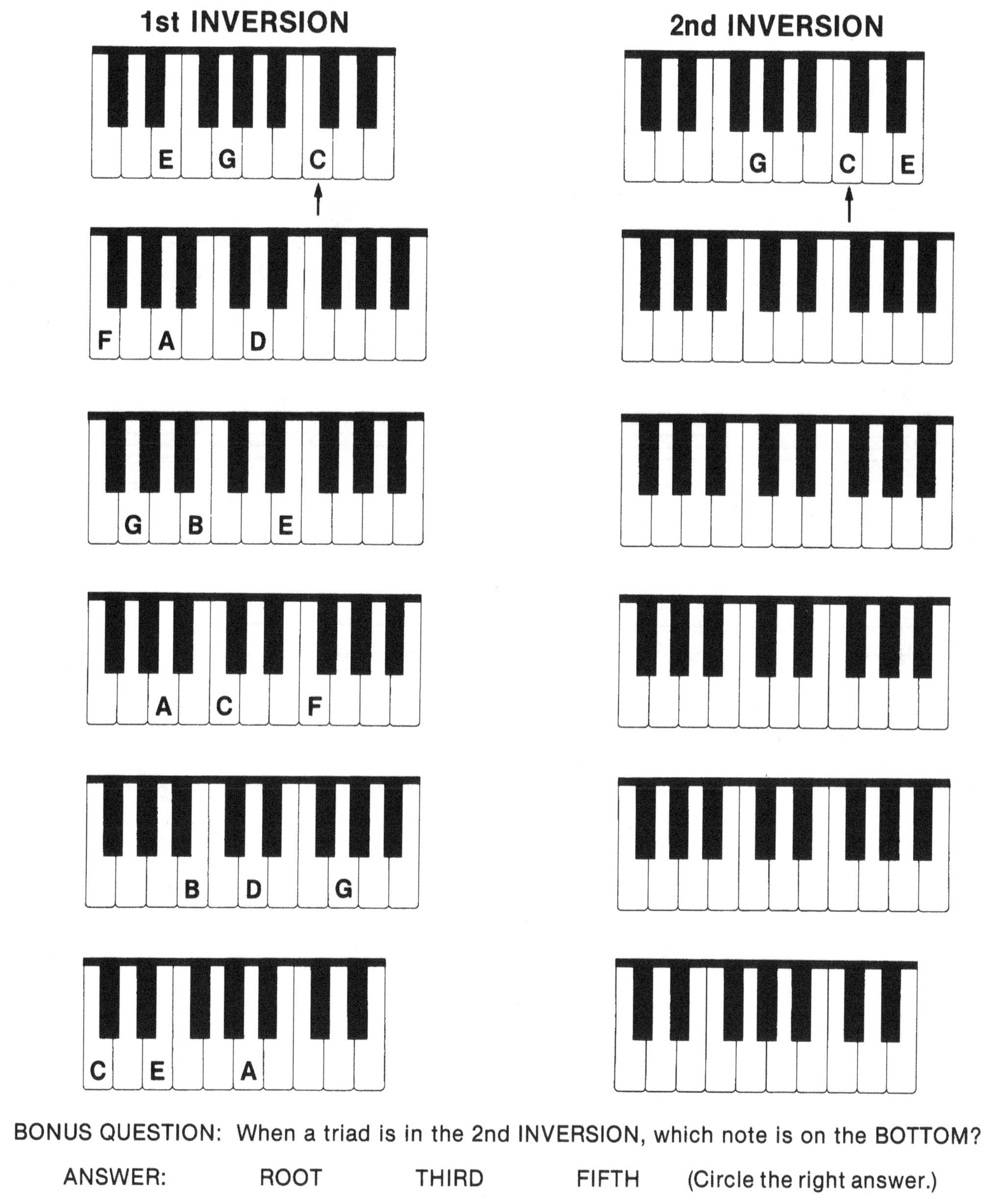

3. BONUS QUESTION: When a triad is in the 2nd INVERSION, which note is on the BOTTOM?

ANSWER: ROOT THIRD FIFTH (Circle the right answer.)

Score 10 for each correct 2nd INVERSION TRIAD. ________
Score 2 for each correct ARROW. ________
Score 30 for BONUS QUESTION. ________
PERFECT SCORE = 100. YOUR SCORE: ________

Assign with pages 42-43.

Triads in All Positions

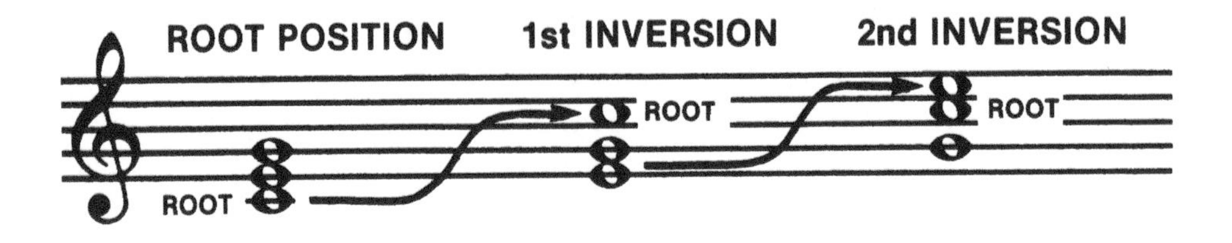

1. In the measure after each ROOT POSITION triad, write the same triad in the 1st INVERSION. In the next measure, write the same triad in the 2nd INVERSION.

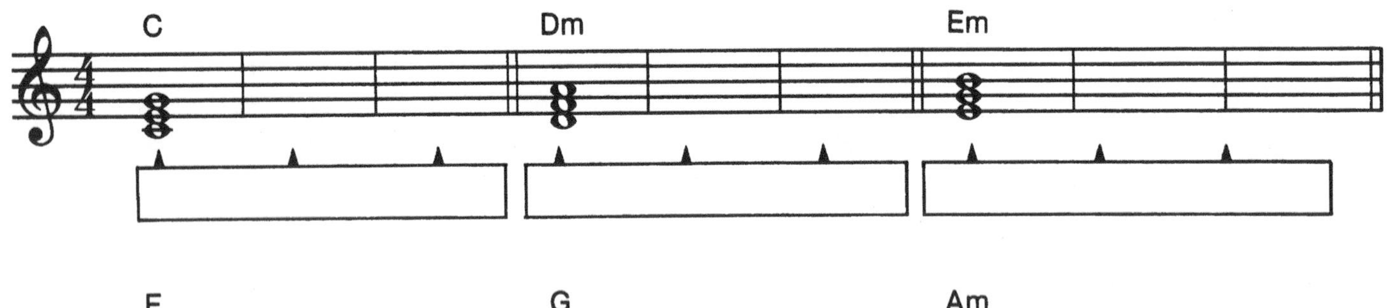

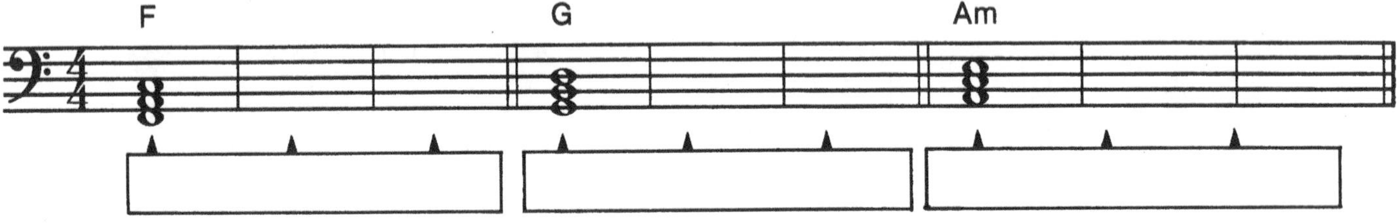

Reviewing: Major & Minor Triads

MAJOR TRIADS in ROOT POSITION consist of a ROOT, a MAJOR 3rd (4 half steps above the root) and a PERFECT 5th (7 half steps above the root).

MINOR TRIADS in ROOT POSITION consist of a ROOT, a MINOR 3rd (3 half steps above the root) and a PERFECT 5th (7 half steps above the root).

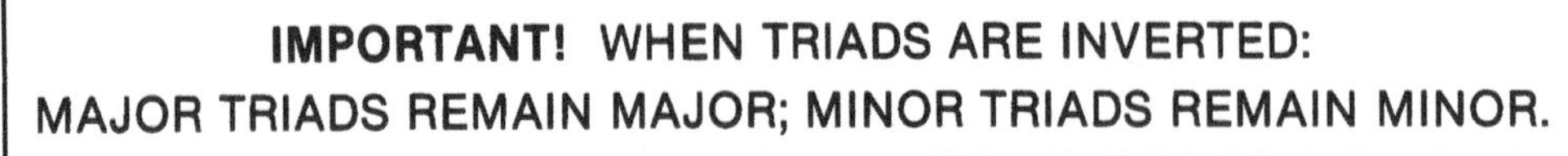

IMPORTANT! WHEN TRIADS ARE INVERTED:
MAJOR TRIADS REMAIN MAJOR; MINOR TRIADS REMAIN MINOR.

2. In No. 1 above, write "MAJOR TRIADS" or "MINOR TRIADS" in the boxes below each group of 3 triads.
3. Play the TOP LINE of No. 1 with the RH.
4. Play the BOTTOM LINE of No. 1 with the LH.

Inverting Major & Minor Triads

Assign with pages 42-43.

Each triad in the left column is in ROOT POSITION.
The TOP 3 triads are MAJOR TRIADS. The bottom 3 are MINOR TRIADS.

1. Write the letter names on each keyboard in the middle column, showing the same triads in the 1st INVERSION.
2. Write the letter names on each keyboard in the right column, showing the same triads in the 2nd INVERSION.
3. Draw arrows pointing UP to the ROOT of each triad.

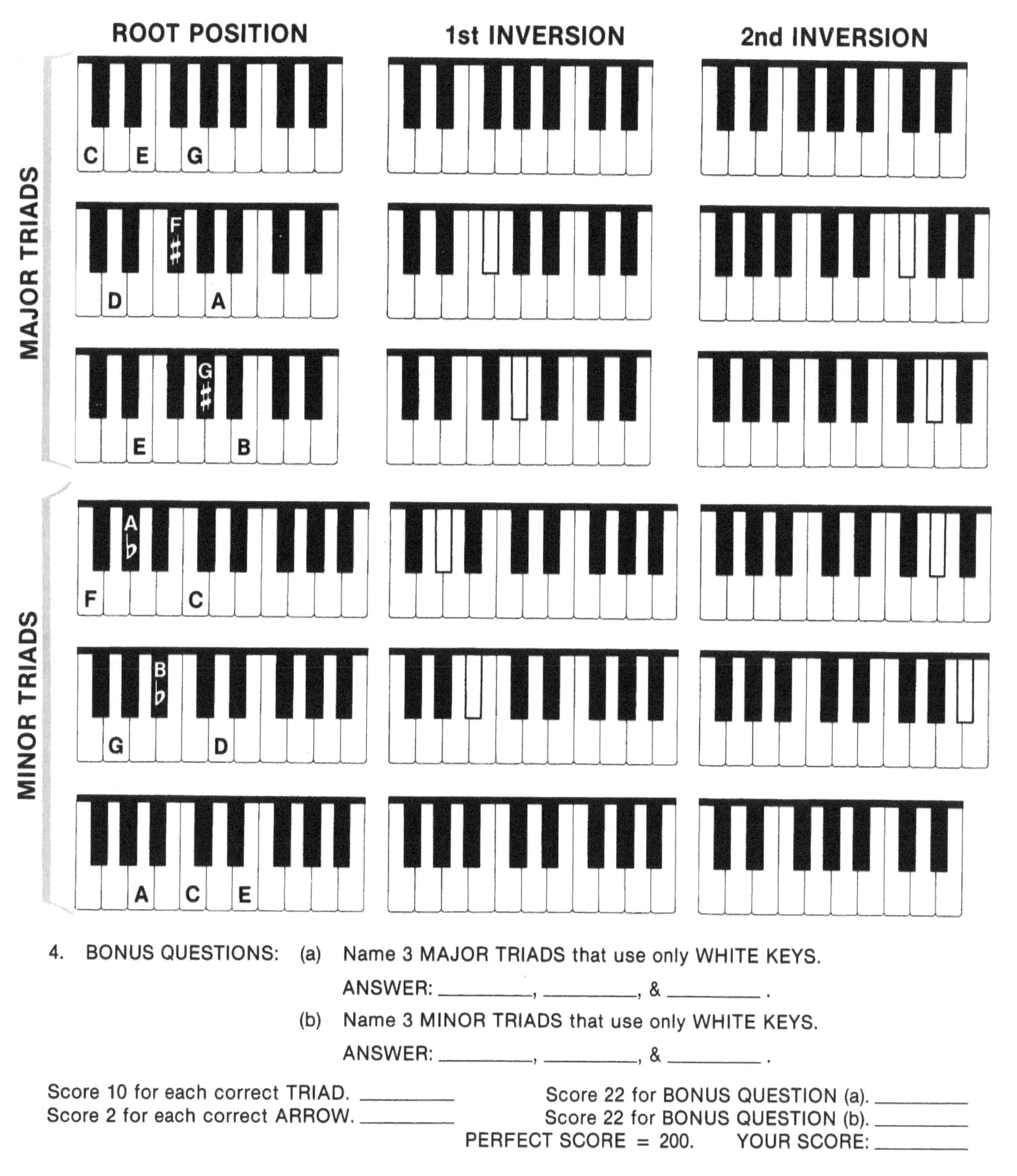

4. BONUS QUESTIONS: (a) Name 3 MAJOR TRIADS that use only WHITE KEYS.

   ANSWER: ________, ________, & ________ .

   (b) Name 3 MINOR TRIADS that use only WHITE KEYS.

   ANSWER: ________, ________, & ________ .

Score 10 for each correct TRIAD. ________
Score 2 for each correct ARROW. ________
Score 22 for BONUS QUESTION (a). ________
Score 22 for BONUS QUESTION (b). ________
PERFECT SCORE = 200. YOUR SCORE: ________

Assign with pages 44-45.

Two-Part Writing

Sometimes 2 melodies with different time values must be written on the same staff.

The UPPER melody (usually called the principal melody) is written with the stems UP.
The LOWER melody (usually called the counter-melody) is written with the stems DOWN.

This is called TWO-PART WRITING. When both melodies have the same note, the stems must point in both directions.

1. PLAY WITH TWO HANDS. Play notes with stems UP with the RH.
   Play notes with stems DOWN with the LH.

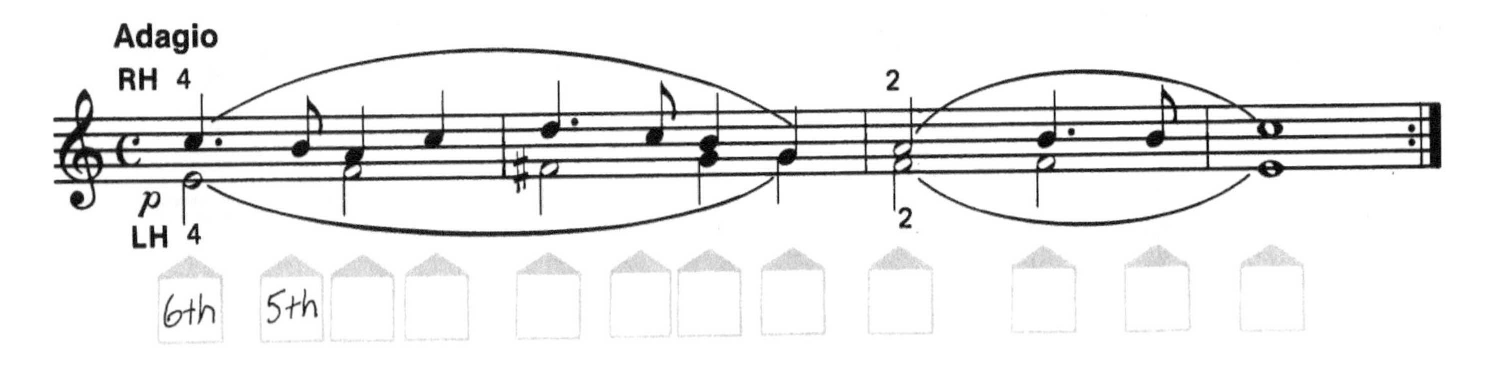

2. In the boxes above, write the name of each HARMONIC INTERVAL produced by the 2 parts, as shown in the 1st two examples. (The 5th is an interval because the E is held for two beats.) When both parts have the same note, write S (same).

If the LH has to play something else, the RH may be required to play 2 parts in the treble clef.In the music below, the 2 parts can be easily played with the RH by using the THUMB on the LOWER NOTES.

3. PLAY WITH RH ONLY.

In the following example, 2 more parts have been added for the LH.

4. PLAY WITH BOTH HANDS. Play the 2 upper parts with the RH.
   Play the 2 lower parts with the LH.

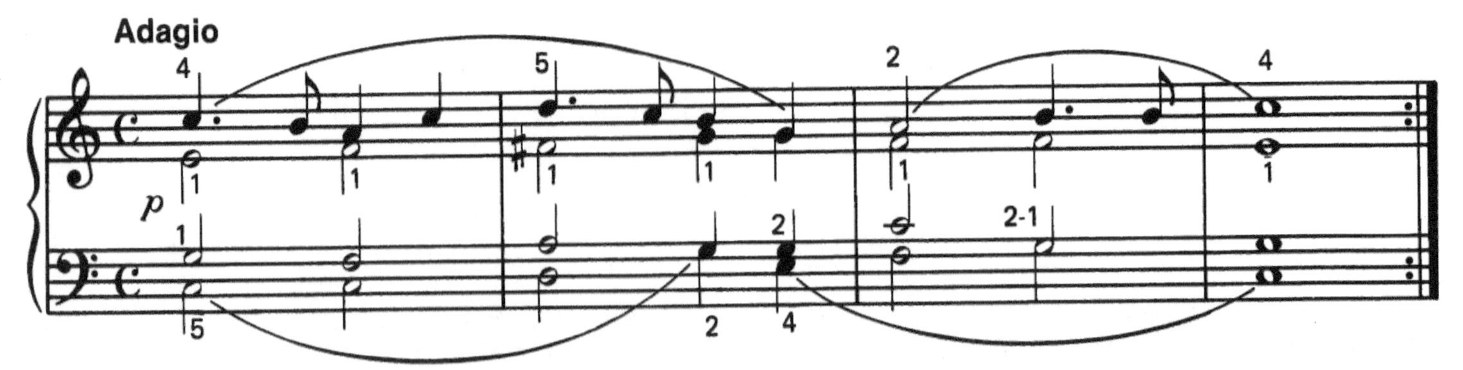

Assign with pages 46-47.

Seventh Chord Review

A SEVENTH CHORD has 4 notes, a series of 3rds stacked one above the other:

A SEVENTH CHORD may be built by adding a 3rd above any root position triad:

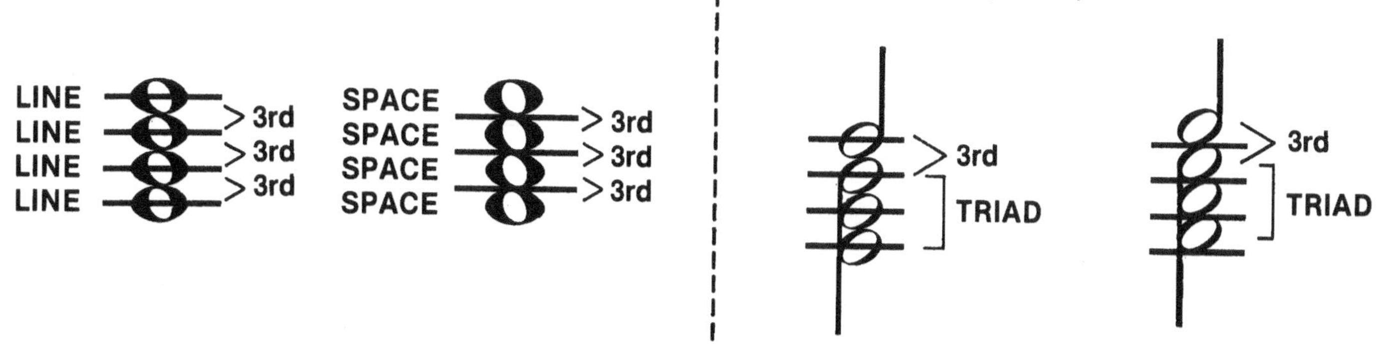

It is best to consider the SEVENTH CHORD as a TRIAD (root, 3rd, 5th) with the added note a 7th ABOVE THE ROOT, since that is the reason it is called a 7th chord.

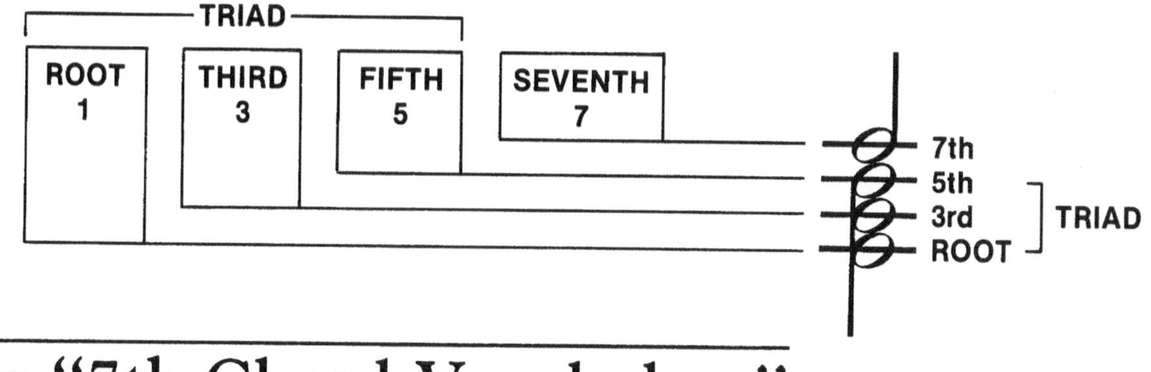

The "7th Chord Vocabulary"

When 7th CHORDS are spelled in ROOT POSITION, always skip ONE LETTER of the MUSICAL ALPHABET between each note. This gives you the following basic **7th CHORD VOCABULARY:**

A C E G B D F A C E G B D F A C E G B D F A C E G B D F

The sharps or flats included in the 7th chords spelled with these letters will depend on the key signature of the music you are playing.

1. Complete each column by adding the note-names of the 3rd, 5th & 7th above each given root, as shown in the 1st column.
2. Play each of these basic 7th chords, using RH 1 2 3 5. Play them again, using LH 5 3 2 1.

	7th	G						
TRIAD	5th	E						
	3rd	C						
	Root	A	B	C	D	E	F	G

V7 Chords in All Positions

Assign with pages 48–51.

The V7 CHORD is built on the 5th note of the scale.
The V7 CHORD is formed from a MAJOR TRIAD with a note added that is a 7th above the ROOT.
The V7 CHORD may be played in the following positions.

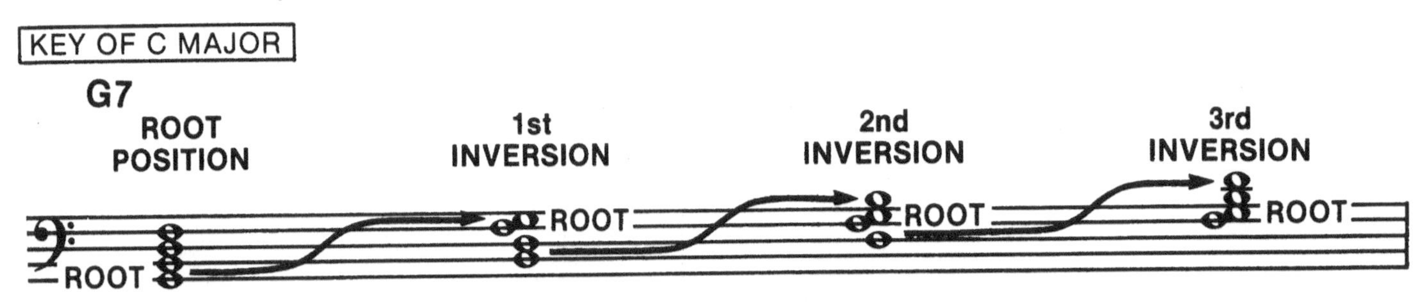

The 5th is *often* omitted from the V7 chord. The 3rd is *sometimes* omitted instead.
When a note is omitted from the chord, it will have only three positions.

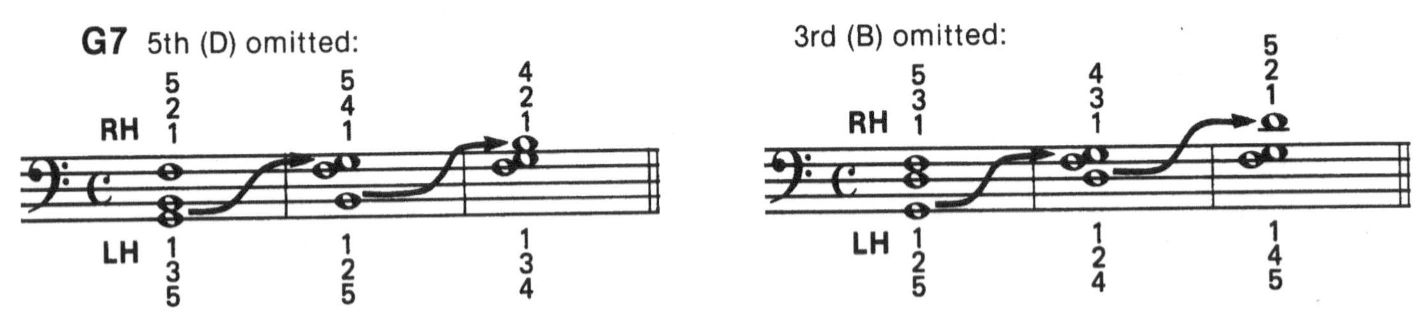

1. Play the above G7 CHORDS, 1st with the LH, as written, then with the the RH, one octave higher than written.

The V7 CHORDS in the following examples are given in the ROOT POSITIONS.

2. In the 2 measures following each chord below, write the 2 inversions of the chord.
3. Play, 1st with LH, as written, then with RH, one octave higher.

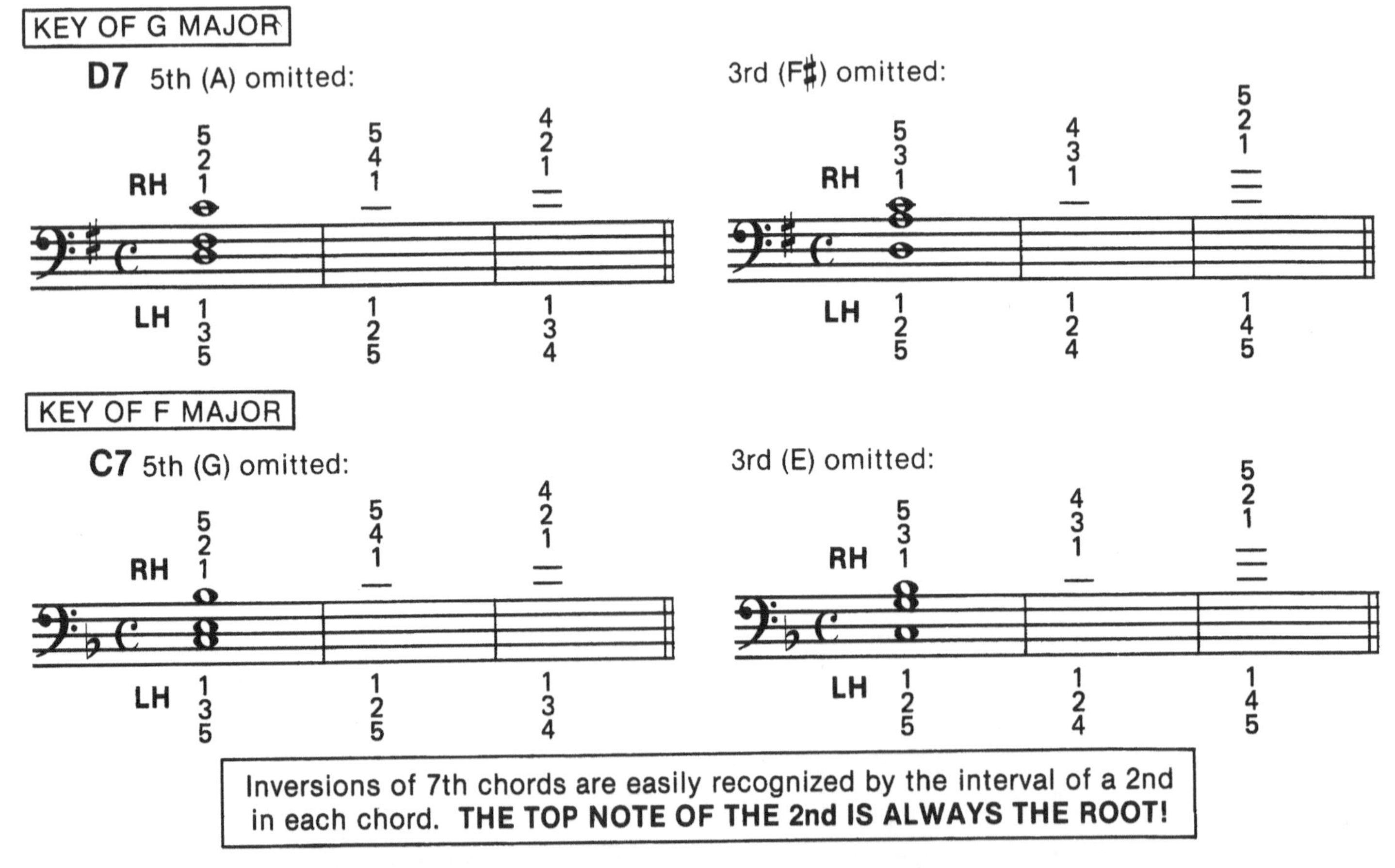

Inversions of 7th chords are easily recognized by the interval of a 2nd in each chord. **THE TOP NOTE OF THE 2nd IS ALWAYS THE ROOT!**

4. Draw an arrow (⟵) pointing to the ROOT of each V7 chord above.

Inverting V7 Chords on the Keyboard

Assign with pages 48–51.

THE CHORDS IN THE LEFT COLUMN ARE V7 CHORDS WITH OMITTED 5ths.

1. Write the letter names on the 2 keyboards in the next 2 columns, showing the 2 inversions of each chord.

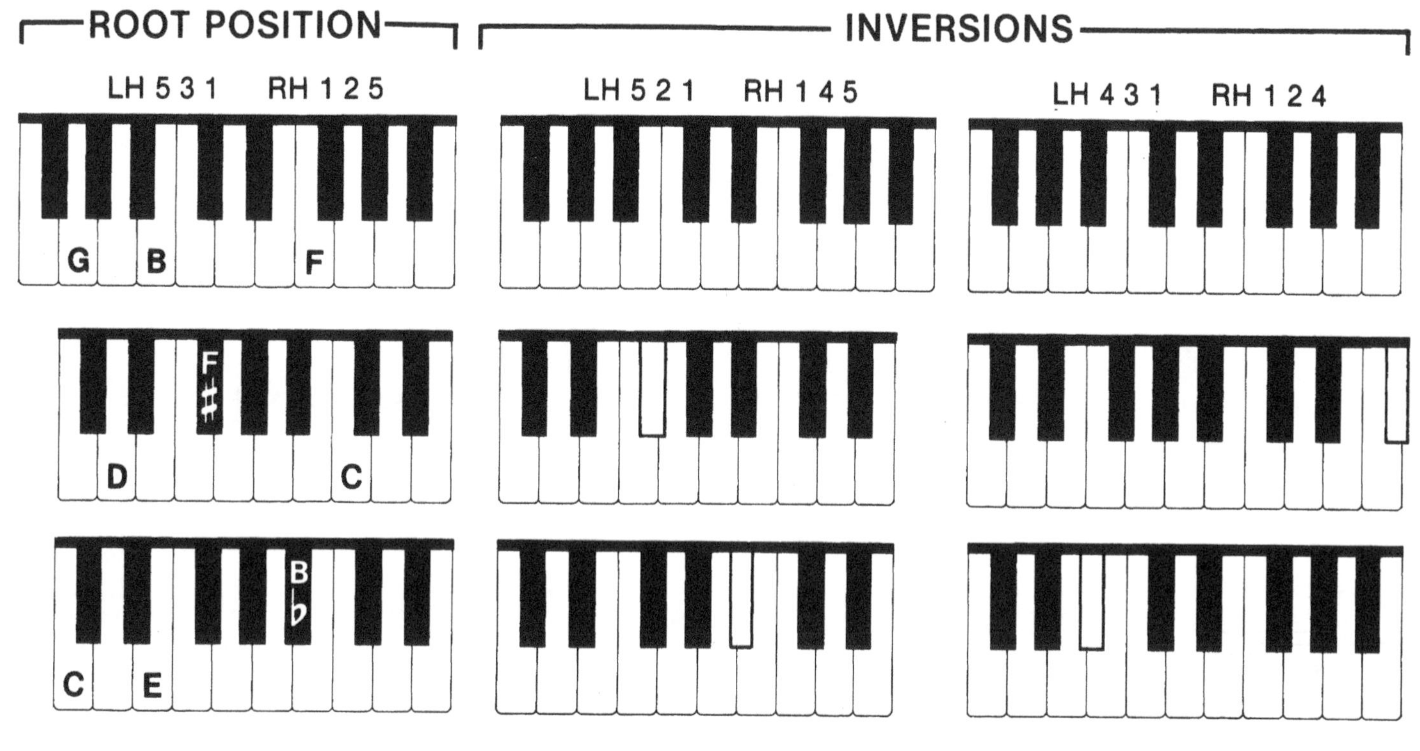

2. PLAY each chord in any convenient place on the keyboard, first with LH, then with RH. Use the fingering shown at the top of each column.

THE CHORDS IN THE LEFT COLUMN ARE V7 CHORDS WITH OMITTED 3rds.

3. Write the letter names on the 2 keyboards in the next 2 columns showing the 2 inversions of each chord.

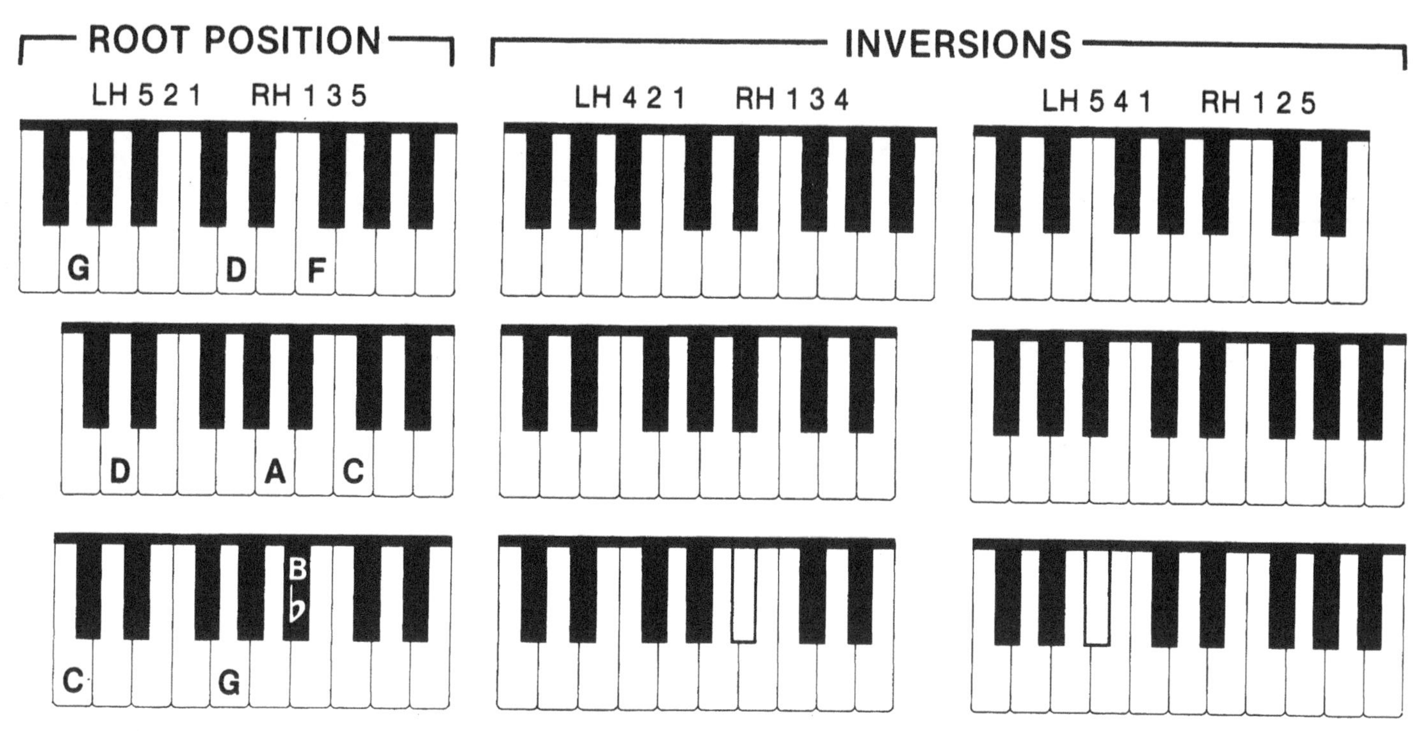

4. PLAY each chord in any convenient place on the keyboard, first with LH, then with RH. Use the fingering shown at the top of each column.

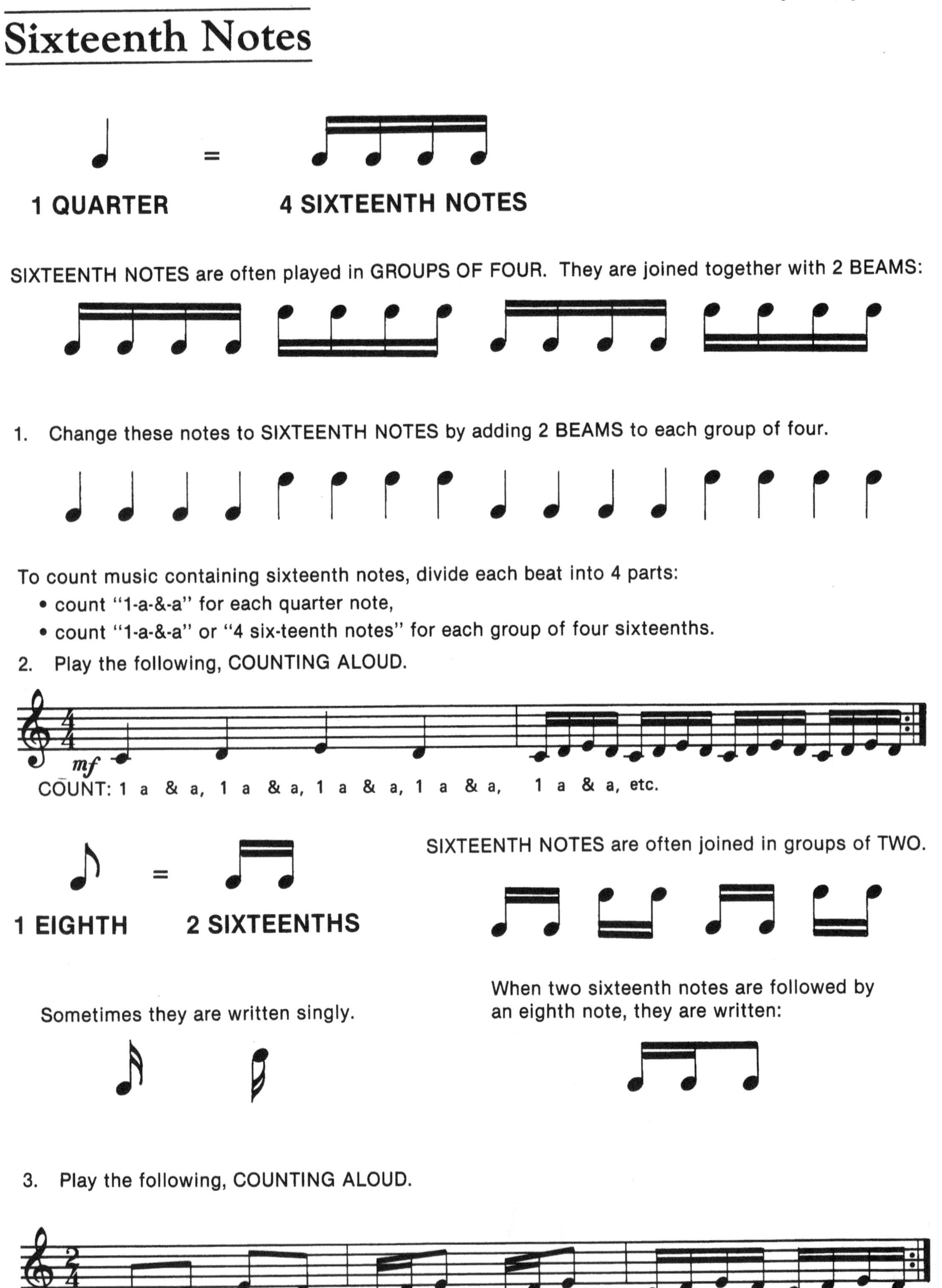

Assign with pages 52-53.

Sixteenth Notes

1 QUARTER = **4 SIXTEENTH NOTES**

SIXTEENTH NOTES are often played in GROUPS OF FOUR. They are joined together with 2 BEAMS:

1. Change these notes to SIXTEENTH NOTES by adding 2 BEAMS to each group of four.

To count music containing sixteenth notes, divide each beat into 4 parts:

- count "1-a-&-a" for each quarter note,
- count "1-a-&-a" or "4 six-teenth notes" for each group of four sixteenths.

2. Play the following, COUNTING ALOUD.

mf

COUNT: 1 a & a, 1 a & a, 1 a & a, 1 a & a, 1 a & a, etc.

1 EIGHTH = **2 SIXTEENTHS**

SIXTEENTH NOTES are often joined in groups of TWO.

Sometimes they are written singly.

When two sixteenth notes are followed by an eighth note, they are written:

3. Play the following, COUNTING ALOUD.

mf

COUNT: 1 a & a, 1 a & a, 1 a & a, 1 a & a, 1 a & a, etc.

Assign with pages 54-57.

Review of Basic Note Values

ONE MEASURE OF COMMON TIME (C or $\frac{4}{4}$ TIME) CAN CONTAIN:

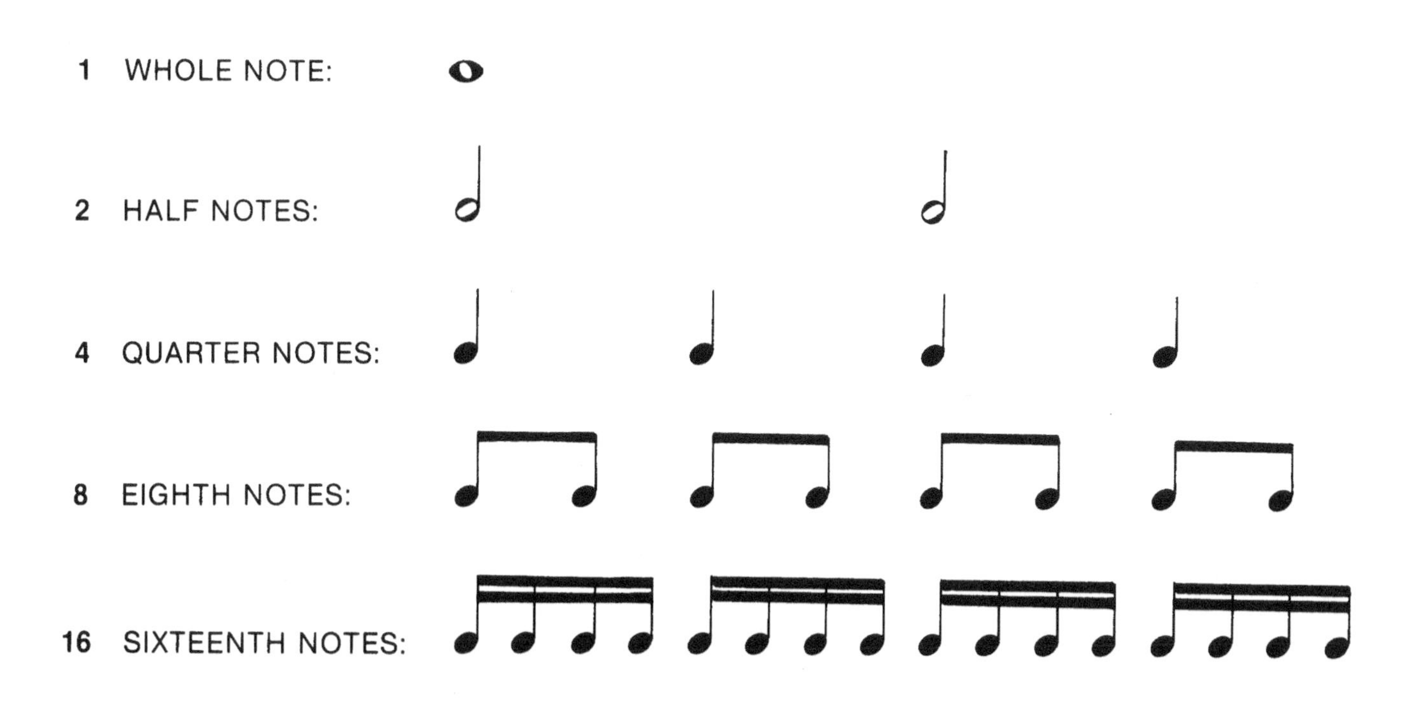

1. Write exactly enough WHOLE NOTES to fill this one measure.

C

2. Write exactly enough HALF NOTES to fill this one measure:

C

3. Write exactly enough QUARTER NOTES to fill this one measure:

C

4. Write exactly enough EIGHTH NOTES to fill this one measure:

C

5. Write exactly enough SIXTEENTH NOTES to fill this one measure:

C

Assign with pages 58-59.

Dotted Eighth Notes

RULE: A DOT AFTER A NOTE INCREASES THE LENGTH OF THE NOTE BY ONE HALF OF ITS VALUE. When a dot appears after a note, play that note as if it were TIED to a note of HALF ITS VALUE:

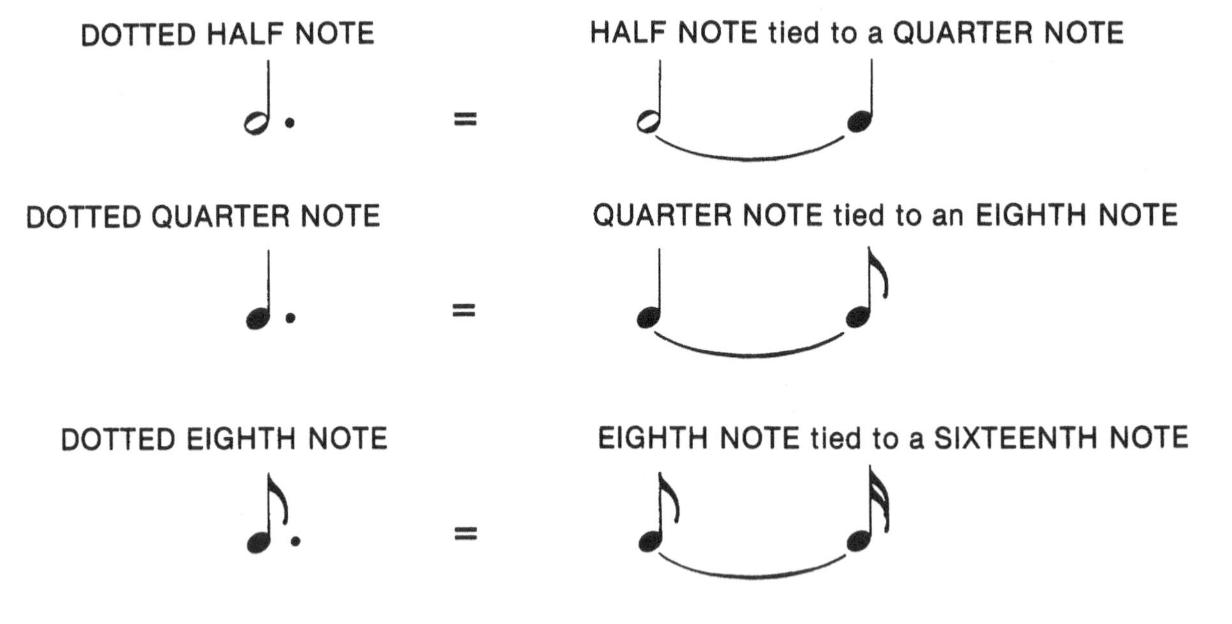

The following 2 lines should sound exactly the same.

1. Play both of the above lines and COUNT ALOUD. The 2 lines should sound exactly the same!
2. Rewrite the following line of music on the staff just below it. Each time an EIGHTH NOTE TIED TO A SIXTEENTH NOTE appears, use a DOTTED EIGHTH NOTE instead.

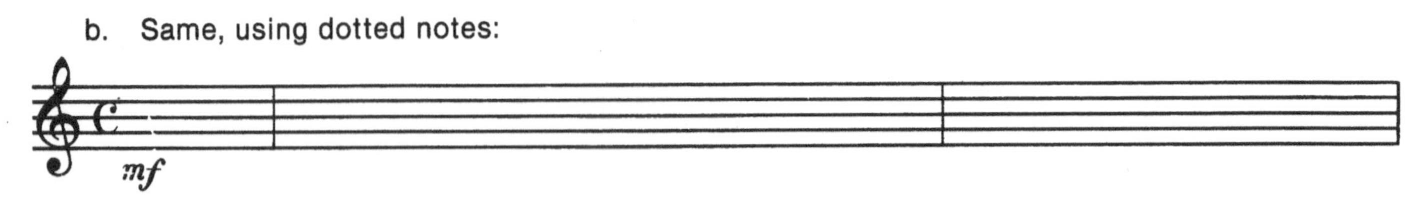

3. Play both of the above lines and COUNT 1 a & a, etc., ALOUD. They should sound exactly the same.

Assign with pages 60-61.

The Key of B♭ Major

1. Write the letter names of the notes of the B♭ MAJOR SCALE, from *left to right,* on the keyboard below. Be sure the WHOLE STEPS & HALF STEPS are correct!

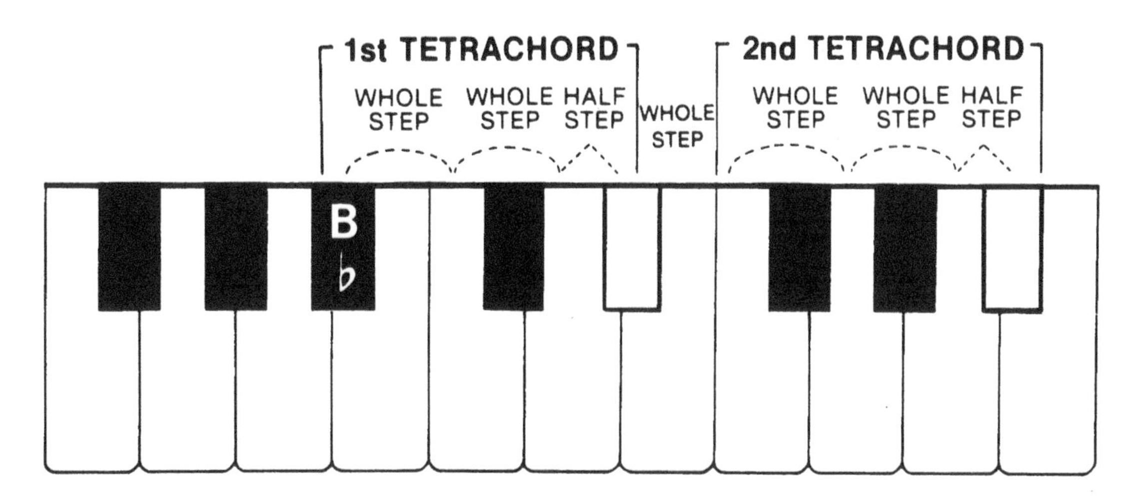

2. Check to be sure you wrote E♭ as the 4th note of the scale. It cannot be called D♯, because scale notes are always in alphabetical order. (You cannot have a scale with two D's and no E's!)

3. Complete the tetrachord beginning on B♭. Write one note over each finger number.

4. Complete the tetrachord beginning on F. Write one note over each finger number.

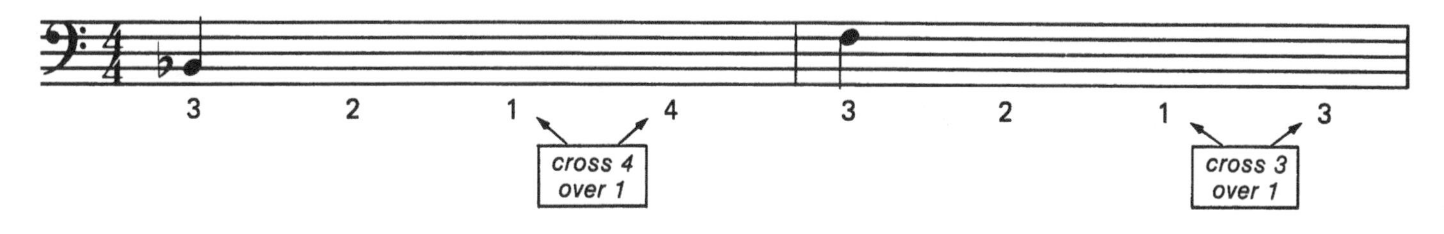

IMPORTANT! ONLY 4 FINGERS ARE USED TO PLAY THE B♭ MAJOR SCALE WITH THE LH AND RH! THE 5th IS NOT USED.

Beginning with LH 3, the scale is fingered in groups of 3 2 1 - 4 3 2 1 ascending.

5. Write the fingering UNDER each note of the following LH scale.

6. Play with LH.

Beginning with RH 4, the fingering groups that follow are 1 2 3 - 1 2 3 4 ascending.

7. Write the fingering OVER each note of the following RH scale.

8. Play with RH.

The Primary Chords in B♭ Major

Assign with pages 62-63.

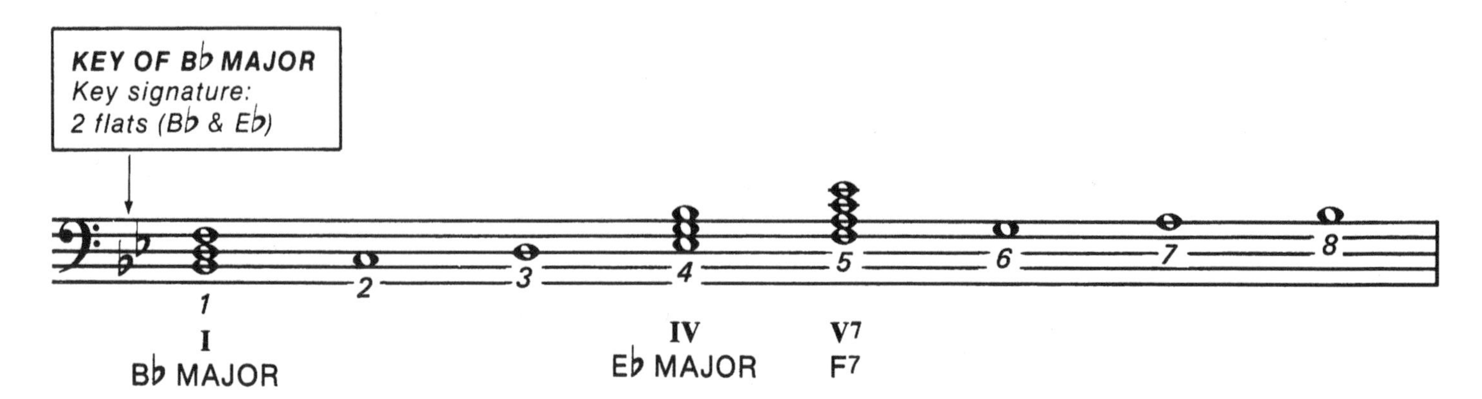

These positions are often used for smooth progressions:

B♭ is the COMMON TONE between **I** & **IV**. **F** is the COMMON TONE between **I** & **V7**.

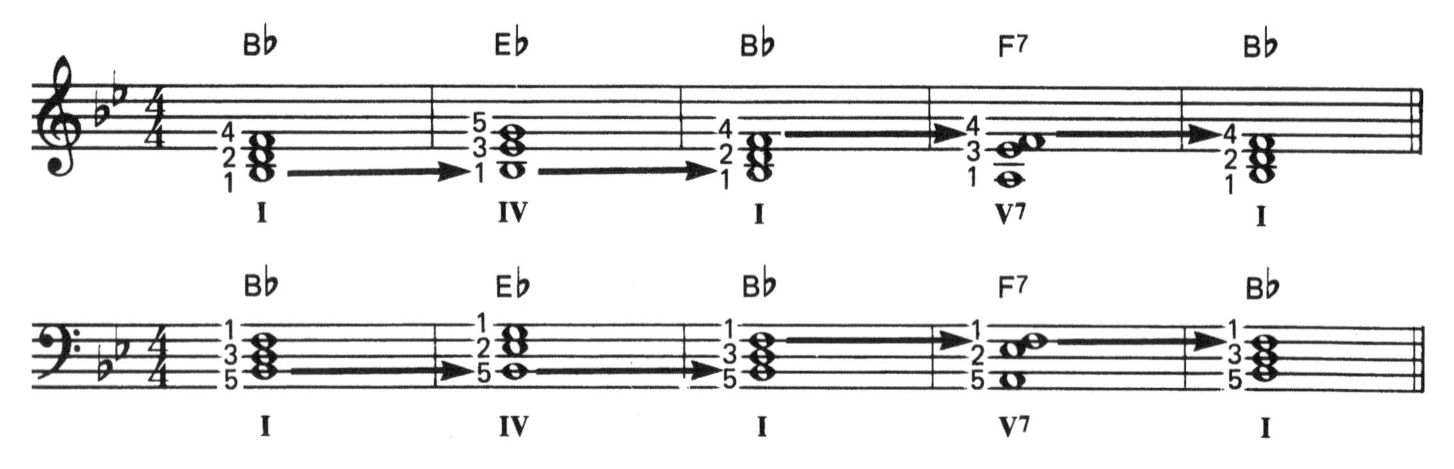

1. Rewrite the above progressions on the following staffs.
2. Add fingering.
3. Add arrows to show the common tones.
4. Play with hands separate.

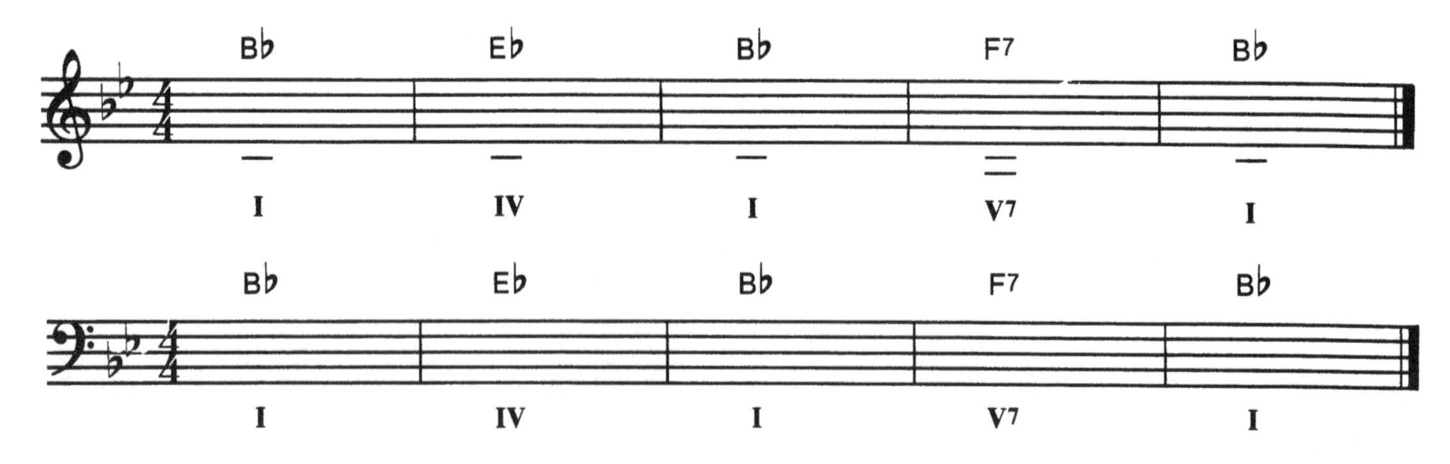

Assign with pages 64-67.

The Primary Chords in B♭ Major—All Positions

1. In the blank measures after each ROOT POSITION chord, write the 2 INVERSIONS of the chord.

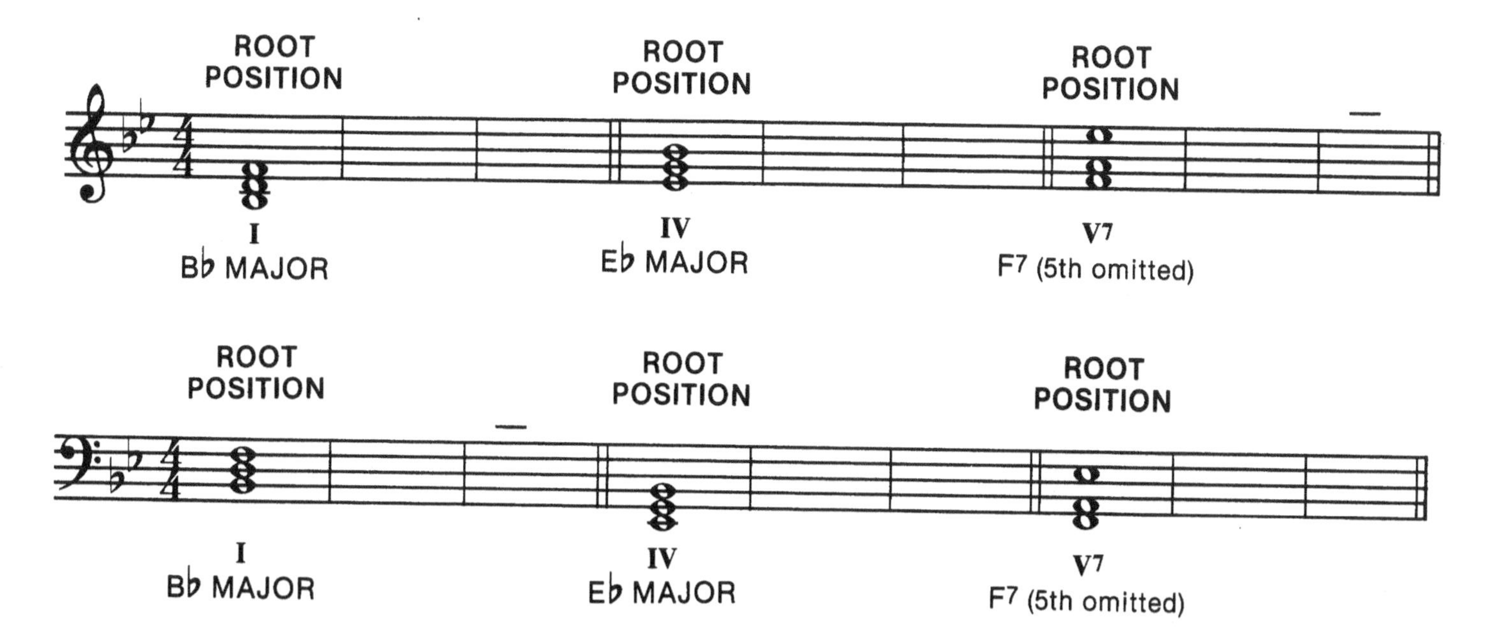

2. On the 2 keyboards to the right of each ROOT POSITION chord, write the letter names showing the 2 inversions of the chord.

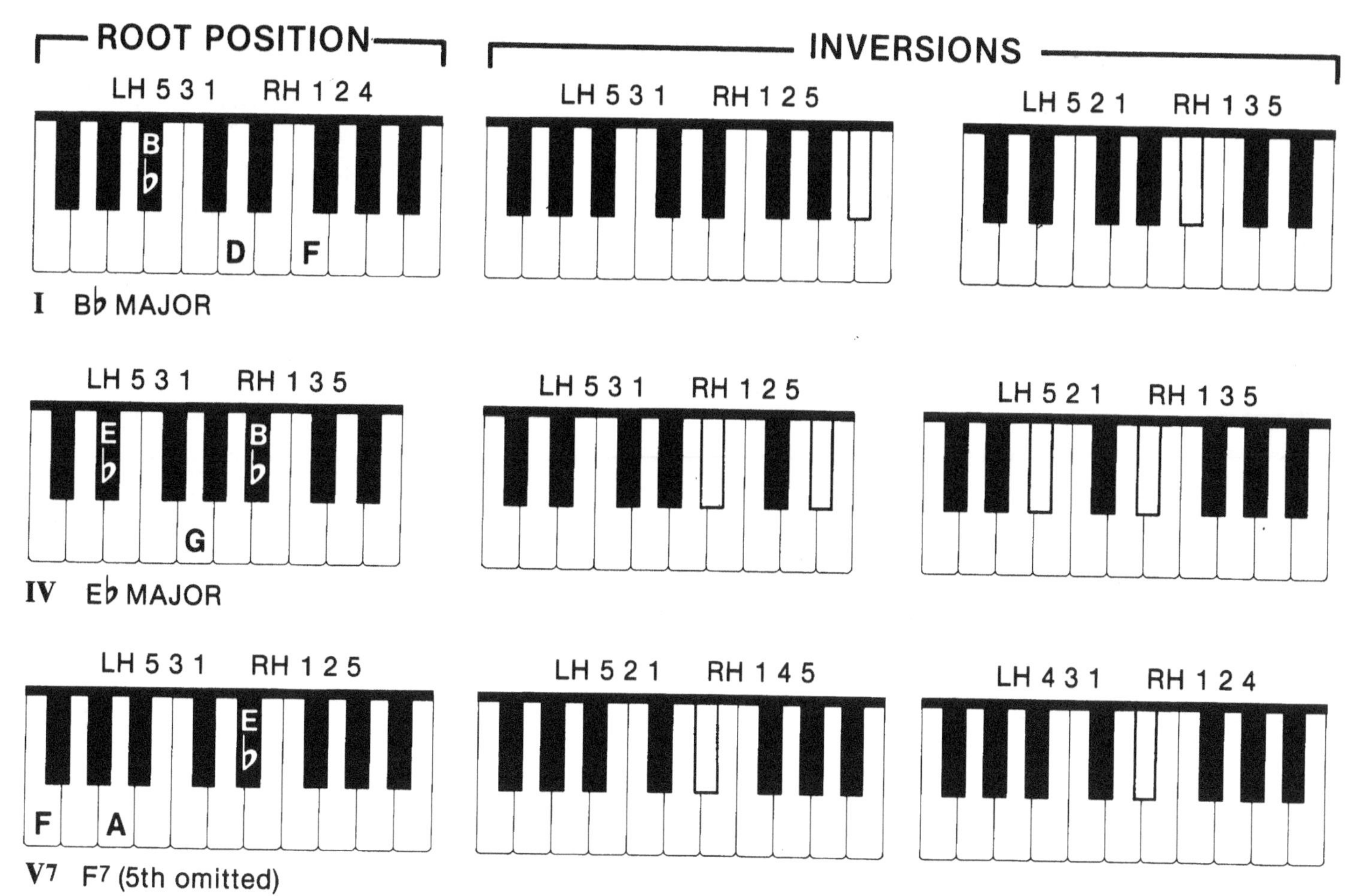

3. Play each chord shown on the above keyboards in any convenient place on your piano, first with LH, then with RH. Use the fingering shown above each keyboard.

The Key of G Minor (Relative of B♭ Major)

G MINOR is the relative of **B♭ MAJOR.**
Both keys have the same key signature (2 flats, B♭ & E♭).
REMEMBER: The RELATIVE MINOR begins on the 6th tone of the MAJOR SCALE.

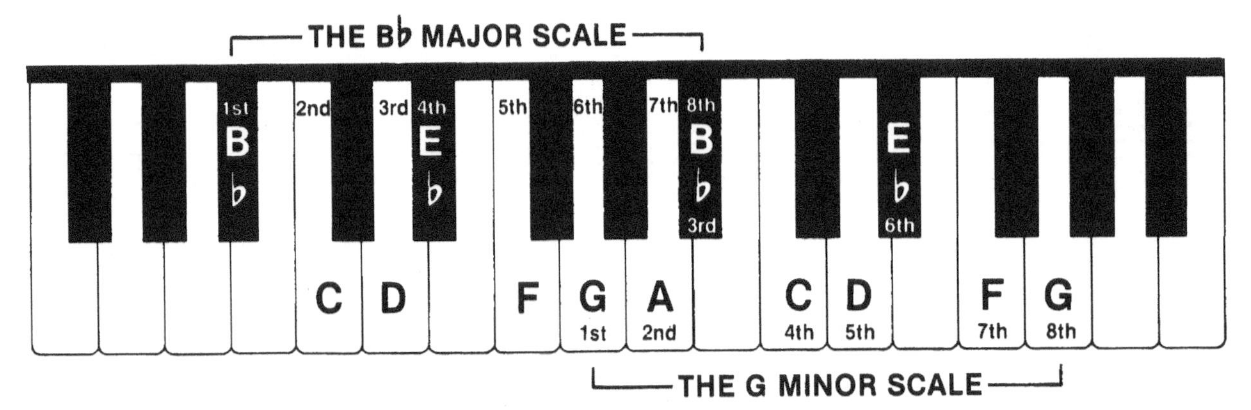

THE NATURAL MINOR SCALE. This scale uses *only* the tones of the relative major scale.
1. Play with hands separate.

THE HARMONIC MINOR SCALE. The 7th tone (F) is raised 1 half step, ASCENDING & DESCENDING.
2. Add accidentals needed to change these NATURAL MINOR scales into HARMONIC MINOR scales.
3. Play with hands separate.

THE MELODIC MINOR SCALE. 6th & 7th tones are raised 1 half step ASCENDING; descends like natural minor. Add the accidentals.

5. Play with hands separate.

6. (OPTIONAL) Play the above scales with hands together.

Assign with pages 70–71.

The Primary Chords in G Minor

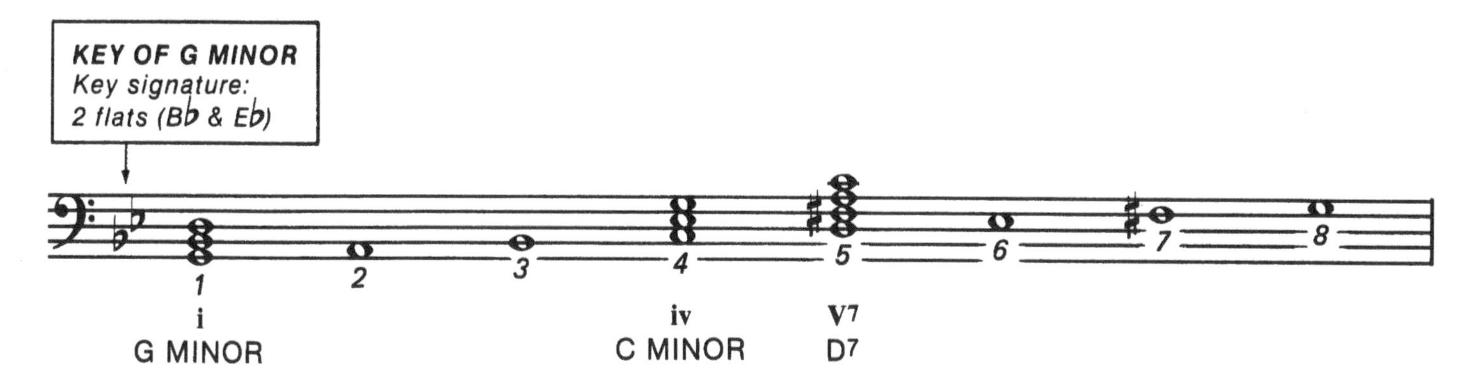

The following positions are often used for smooth progressions:

G is the COMMON TONE between **i** & **iv**. **D** is the COMMON TONE between **i** & **V7**.

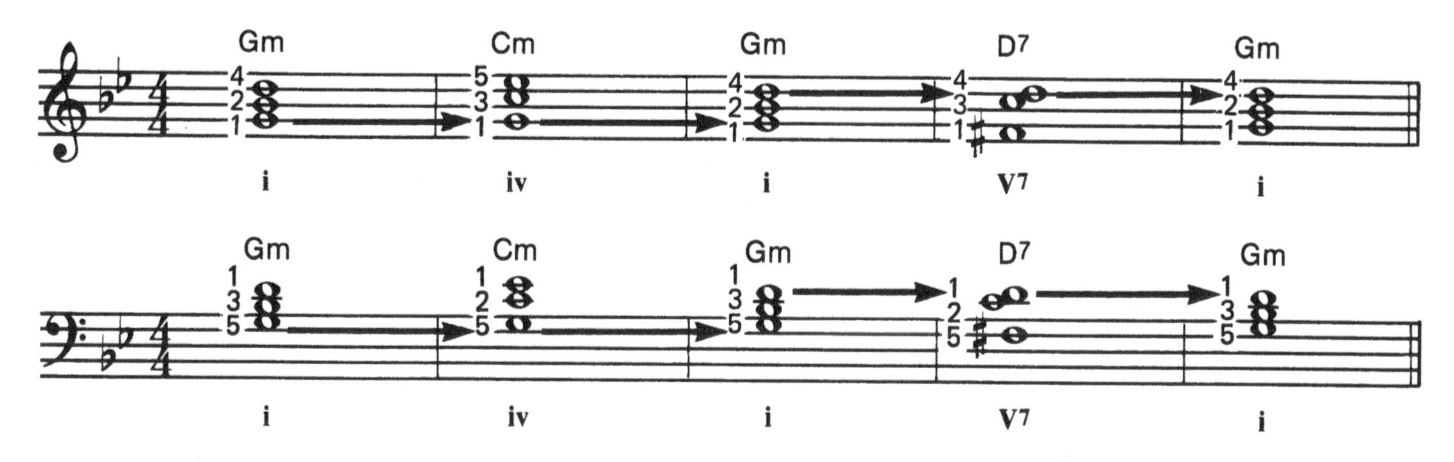

1. Rewrite the above progressions on the following staffs.
2. Add fingering.
3. Add arrows to show the common tones.
4. Play with hands separate.

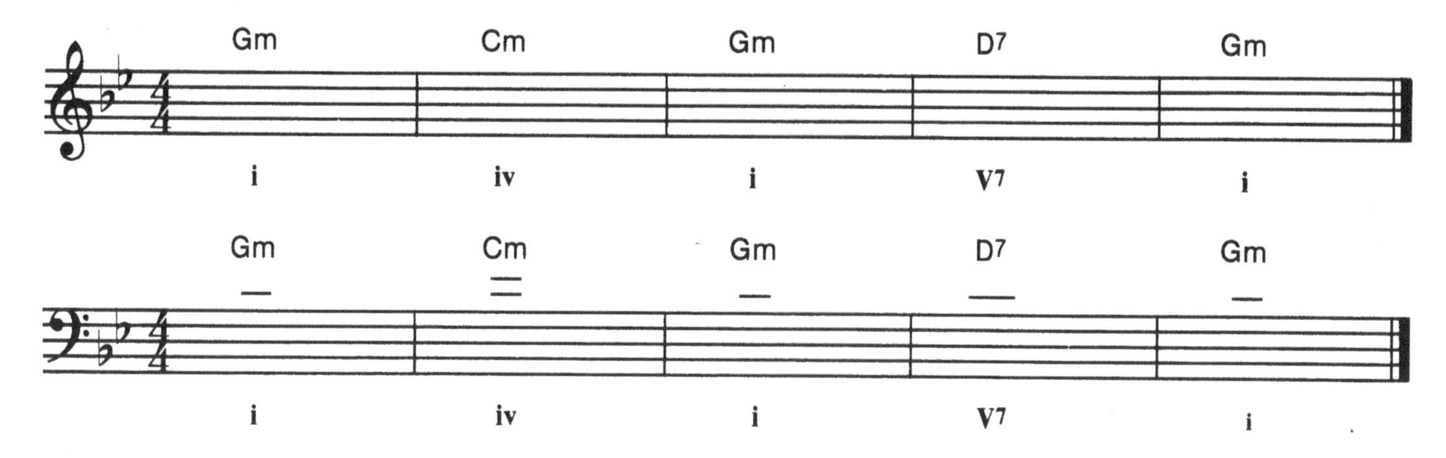

Assign with pages 70–71.

The Primary Chords in G Minor—All Positions

1. In the blank measures after each ROOT POSITION chord, write the 2 INVERSIONS of the chord.

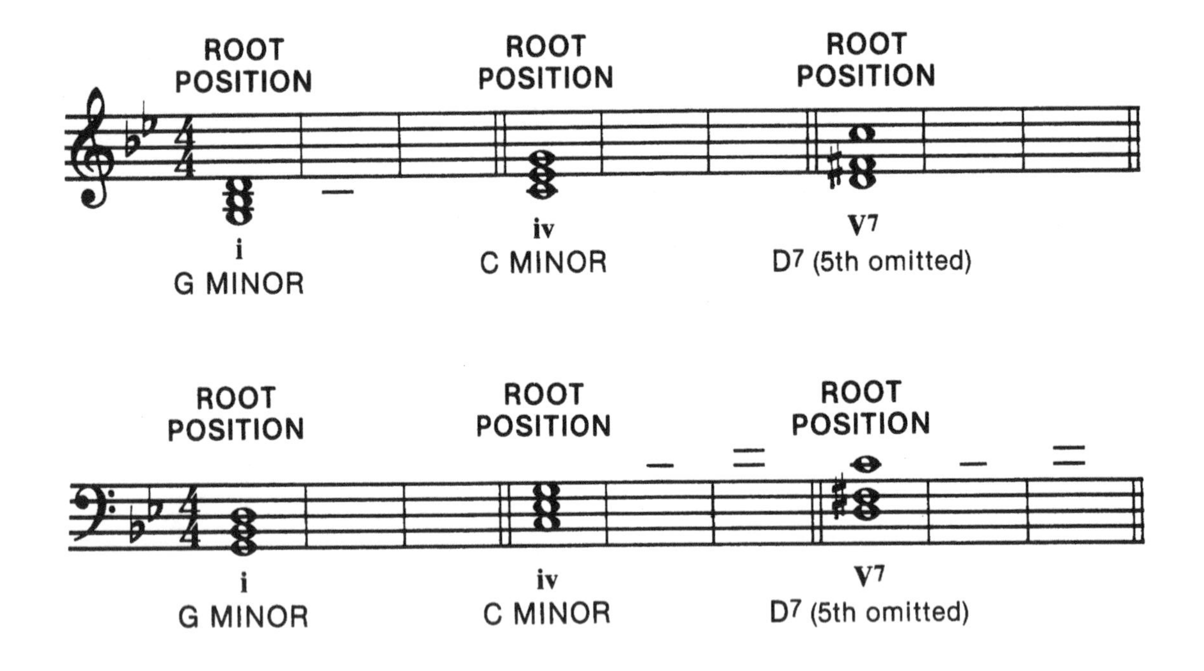

2. On the 2 keyboards to the right of each ROOT POSITION chord, write the letter names showing the 2 INVERSIONS of the chord.

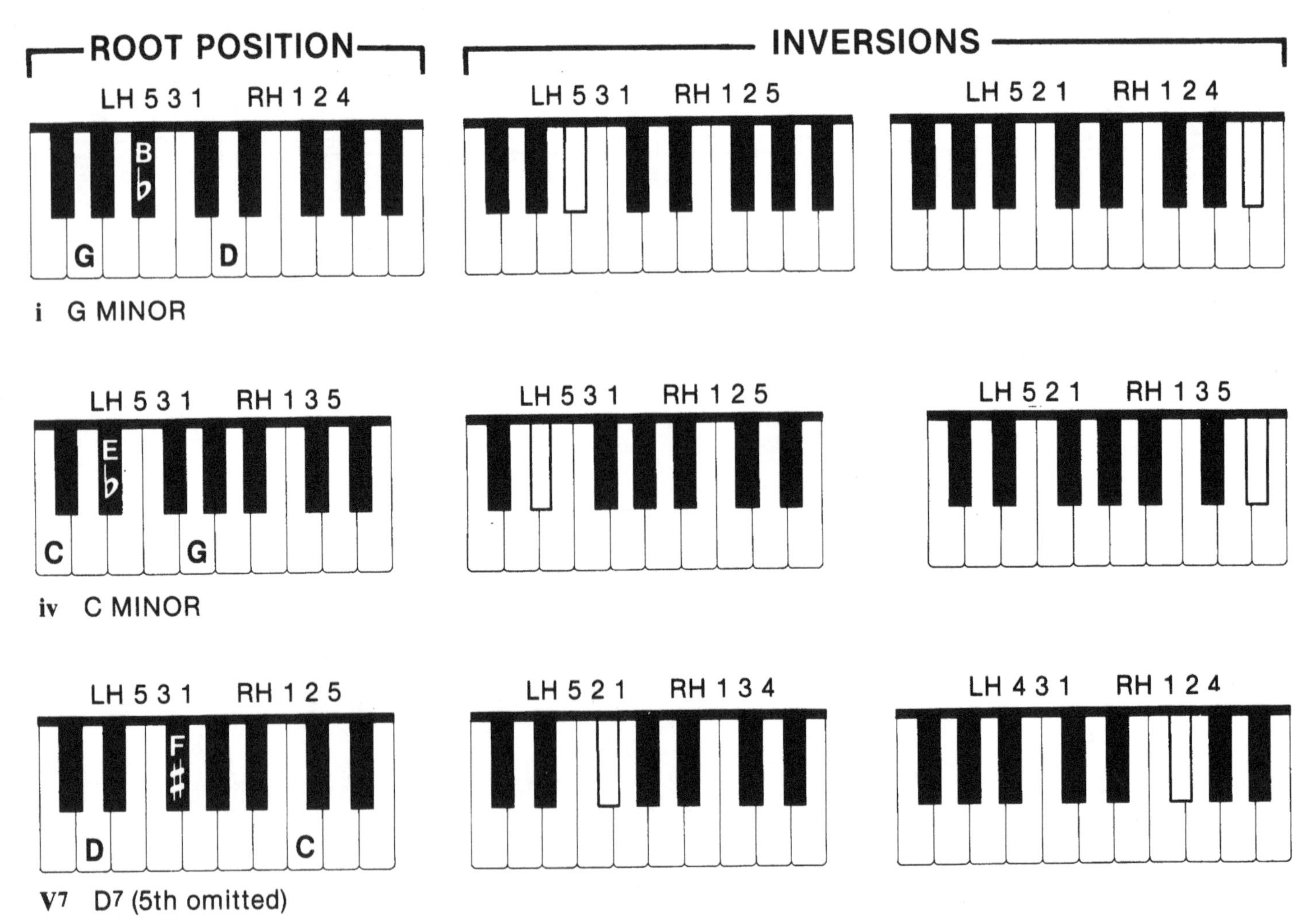

3. Play each chord shown on the above keyboards in any convenient place on your piano, first with LH, then with RH. Use the fingering shown above each keyboard.

Assign with pages 72-73.

Introducing: Diminished Triads

A DIMINISHED TRIAD consists of a ROOT, MINOR 3rd, & DIMINISHED 5th.

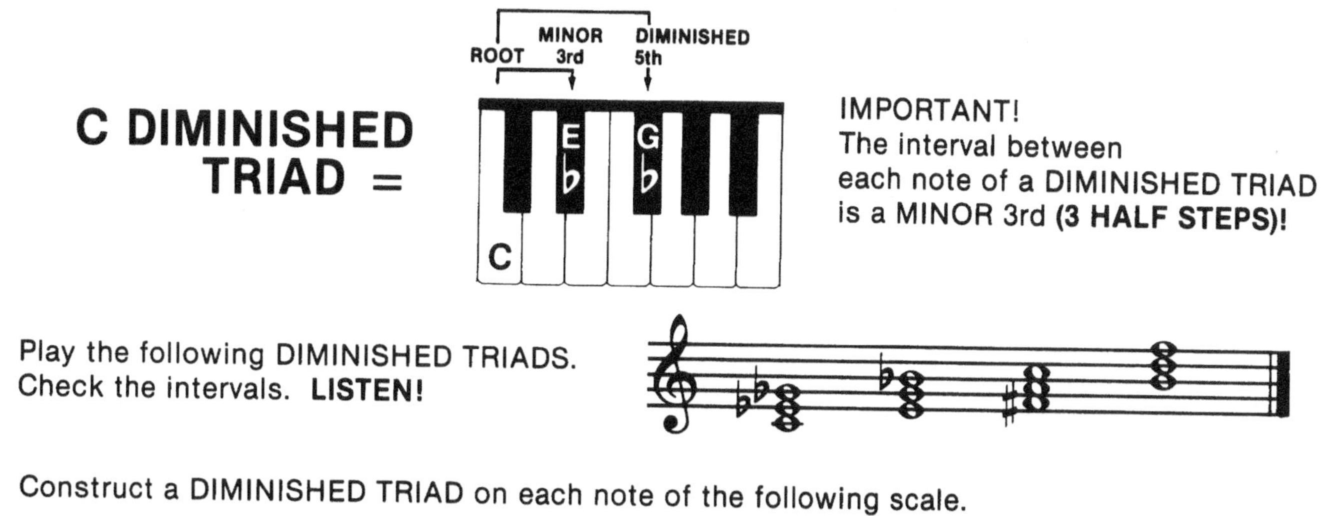

C DIMINISHED TRIAD =

IMPORTANT!
The interval between each note of a DIMINISHED TRIAD is a MINOR 3rd **(3 HALF STEPS)!**

1. Play the following DIMINISHED TRIADS. Check the intervals. **LISTEN!**

2. Construct a DIMINISHED TRIAD on each note of the following scale.

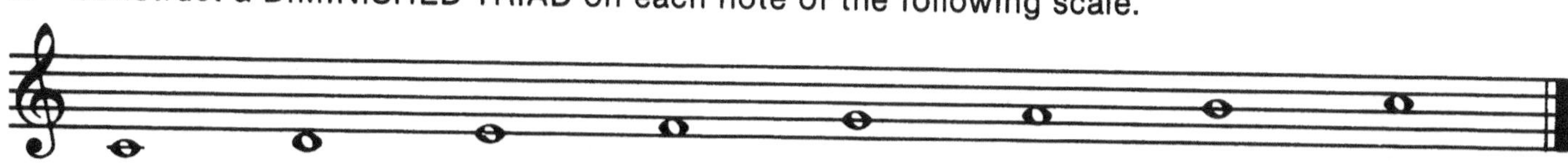

Any MINOR triad may be changed to a DIMINISHED triad by LOWERING the 5th ONE HALF-STEP!

3. Change the 2nd chord in each measure from MINOR to DIMINISHED by lowering the 5th of the chord 1 half step. Use a FLAT sign to lower a natural note, and use a NATURAL sign to lower a sharped note. Remember: accidentals are in effect for a full measure.

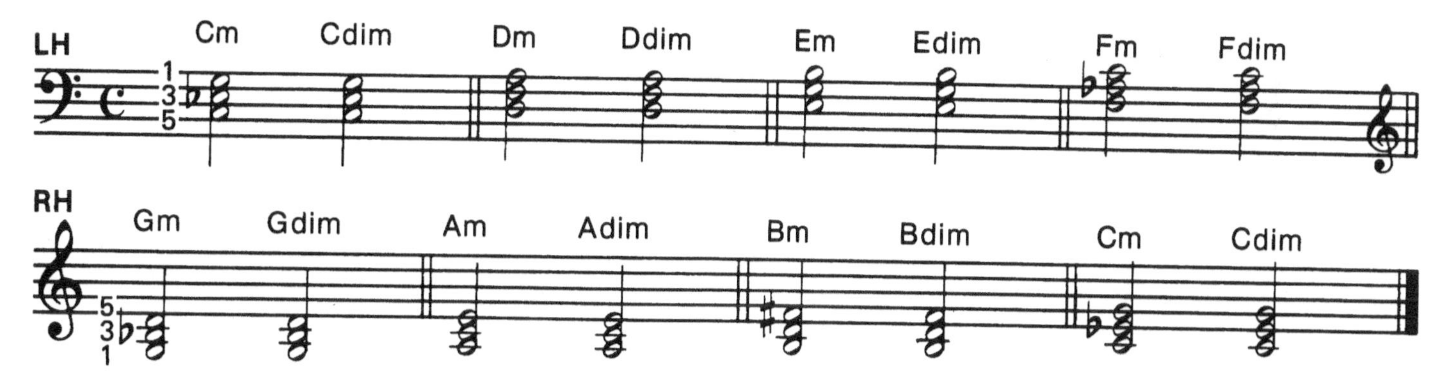

Any MAJOR triad may be changed to a DIMINISHED triad by LOWERING the 3rd & 5th ONE HALF-STEP!

4. Change the 2nd chord in each measure from MAJOR to DIMINISHED by lowering the 3rd and the 5th of each chord 1 half step. Use flats or naturals, or both.

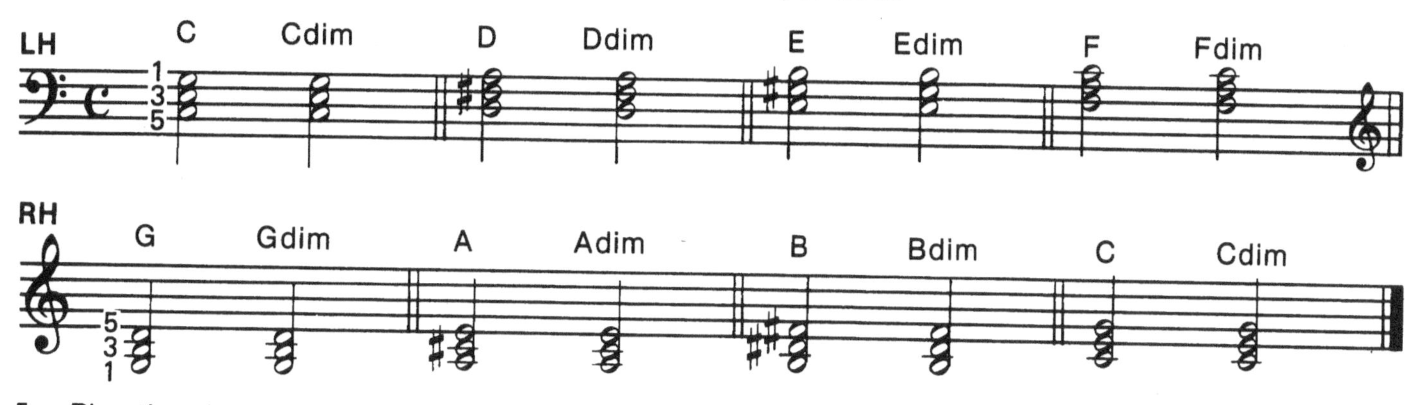

5. Play the above 4 lines of music. Say the name of each chord as you play.

Assign with pages 74–75.

The Double Flat

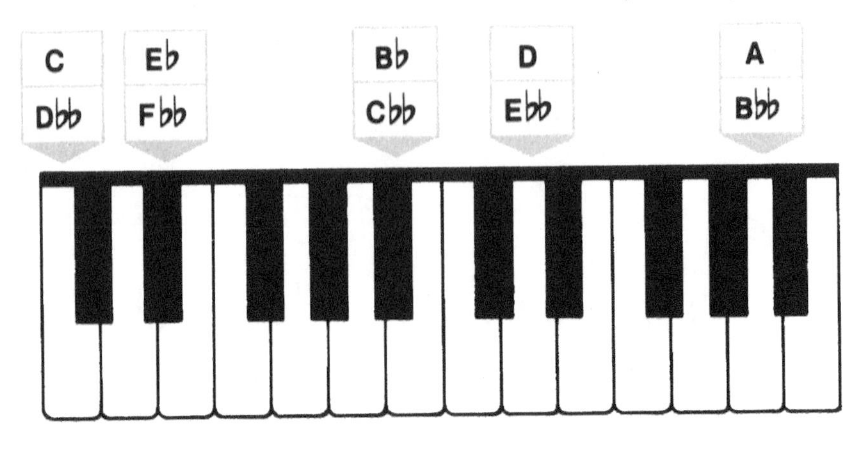

The DOUBLE FLAT (♭♭)
LOWERS a note
2 HALF STEPS (1 whole step)

1. Draw an arrow from each note in the staff to the corresponding key on the keyboard below it, as shown in the first example.

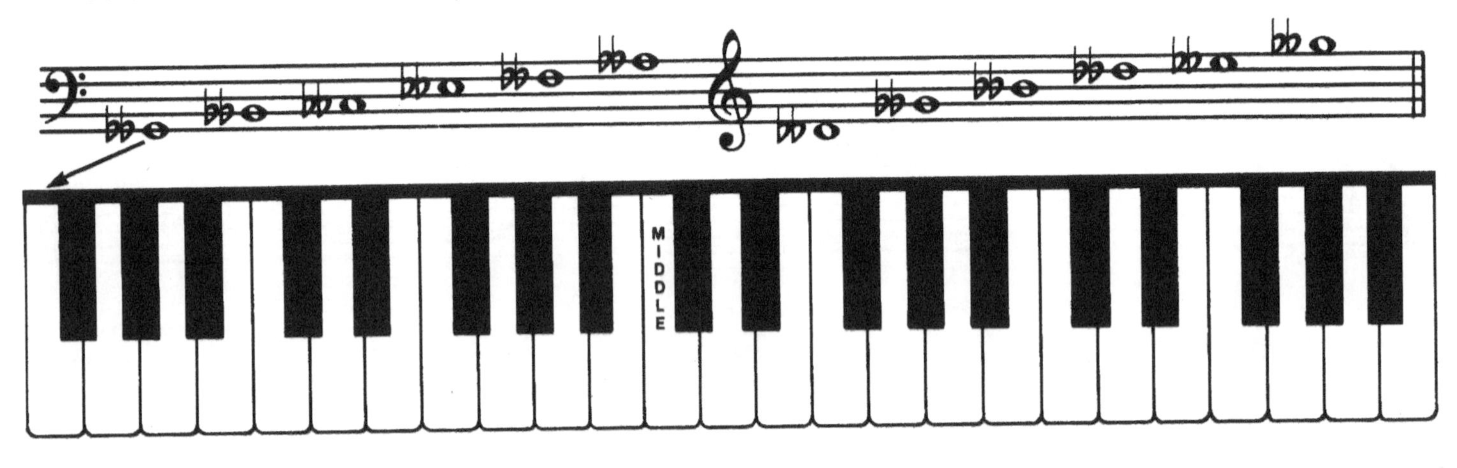

The term **ENHARMONIC** is used for tones that are actually one and the same ON THE KEYBOARD, but are written differently on the staff. Every key has more than one name.

Here are some examples of ENHARMONIC tones:
C♯ & D♭   E♯ & F♮   G♯ & A♭   A♮ & B♭♭

The chart below will show why it is not only CORRECT, but more CONVENIENT to use certain enharmonic spellings of tones.

REMEMBER: In the TRIAD VOCABULARY (see Lesson Book 1, page 64), which makes all triads easy to learn, **ONE LETTER OF THE MUSICAL ALPHABET MUST BE SKIPPED BETWEEN EACH NOTE!**

2. Play the following triads, moving across the columns from left to right. Use R.H. 1 3 5 or L.H. 5 3 1. Say the name of each triad as you play it: "C MAJOR, C MINOR, C DIMINISHED," etc.

MAJOR TRIADS			MINOR TRIADS			DIMINISHED TRIADS		
Root	3rd	5th	Root	3rd (♭)	5th	Root	3rd (♭)	5th (♭)
C	E	G	C	E♭	G	C	E♭	G♭
F	A	C	F	A♭	C	F	A♭	C♭
B♭	D	F	B♭	D♭	F	B♭	D♭	F♭
E♭	G	B♭	E♭	G♭	B♭	E♭	G♭	B♭♭
A♭	C	E♭	A♭	C♭	E♭	A♭	C♭	E♭♭

3. The E♭ MAJOR TRIAD must not be spelled E♭ G A♯. E♭ MINOR must not be spelled E♭ F B♭. E♭ DIMINISHED must not be spelled E♭ G♭ A. Do you understand why?

Introducing: Augmented Triads

Assign with pages 76-77.

The word AUGMENTED means "made larger."
When any MAJOR or PERFECT interval is made larger by 1 half step,
it becomes an AUGMENTED interval.

An AUGMENTED TRIAD consists of a ROOT, MAJOR 3rd, & AUGMENTED 5th.

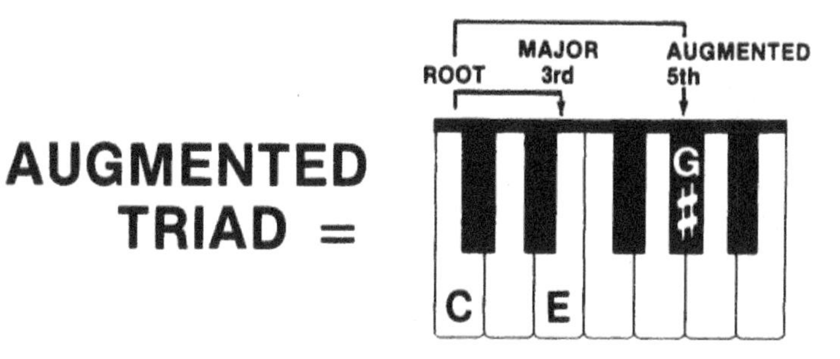

IMPORTANT!
The interval between
each note of an AUGMENTED TRIAD
is a MAJOR 3rd (4 HALF STEPS)!

1. Play the following AUGMENTED TRIADS, using R H 1 3 5.
   Check the intervals. LISTEN as you play.

   The symbol for AUGMENTED is aug or +.

C aug (C+) F aug (F+) G aug (G+)

Any MAJOR triad may be changed to an AUGMENTED triad by raising the 5th ONE HALF-STEP!

2. Change the 2nd chord in each measure from MAJOR to AUGMENTED by raising the 5th of each chord 1 half step. To raise a natural note, use a SHARP sign. To raise a flatted note, use a NATURAL sign.

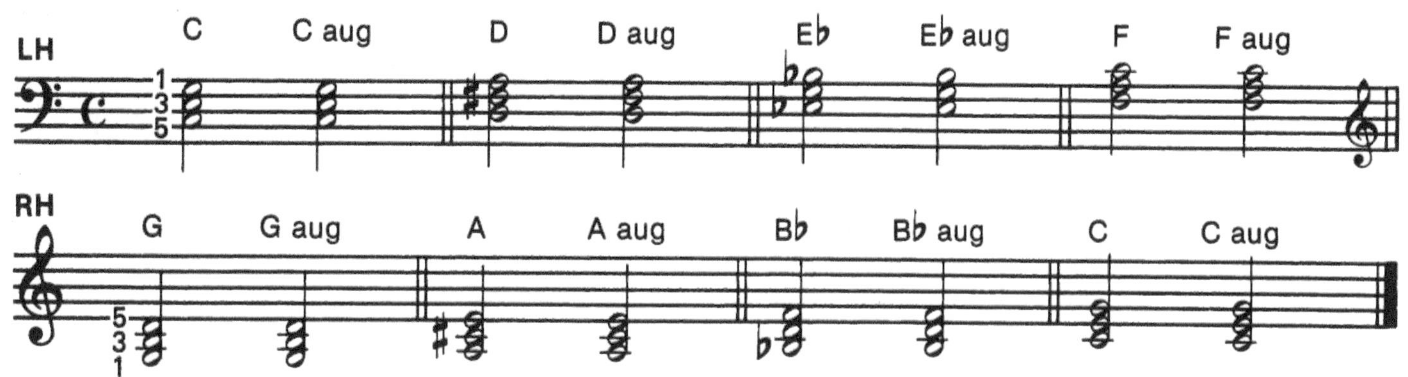

3. Play the above 2 lines of music. Say the name of each triad as you play.
4. Write the name of each triad in the box below it. Use M for MAJOR, m for MINOR, ° for DIMINISHED, and + for AUGMENTED, as shown in the first 5 boxes.

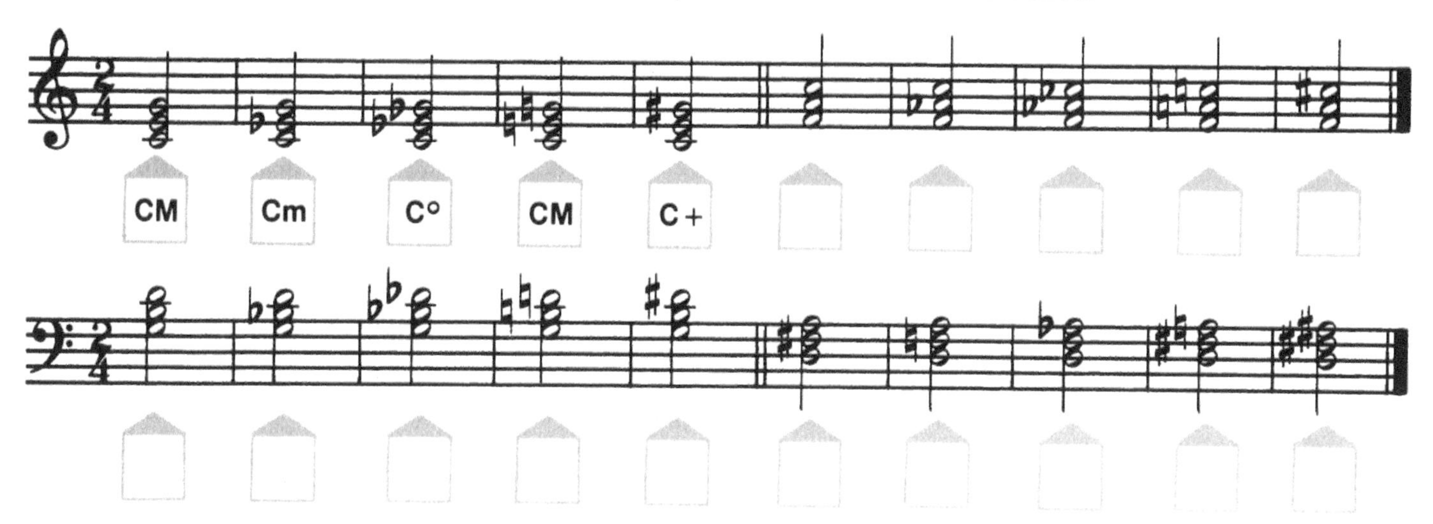

5. Play the above 2 lines with R H 1 3 5 or L H 5 3 1, saying the name of each triad as you play.

Assign with pages 76–77.

The Double Sharp

THE DOUBLE SHARP (𝄪)
RAISES a note
2 HALF STEPS (1 whole step)

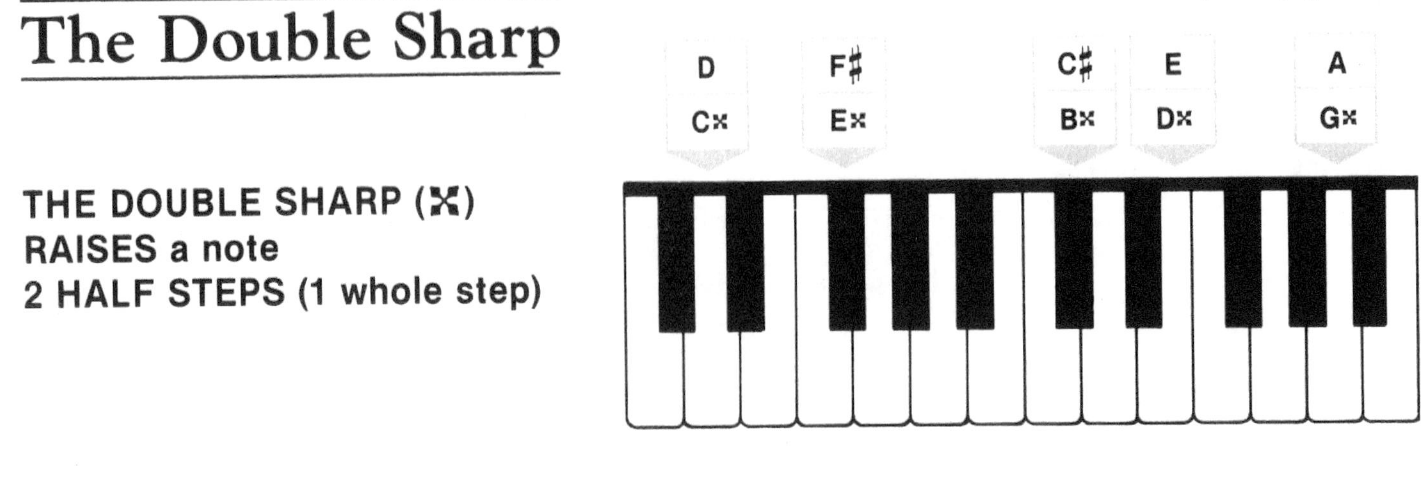

1. Draw an arrow from each note in the staff to the corresponding key on the keyboard below it.

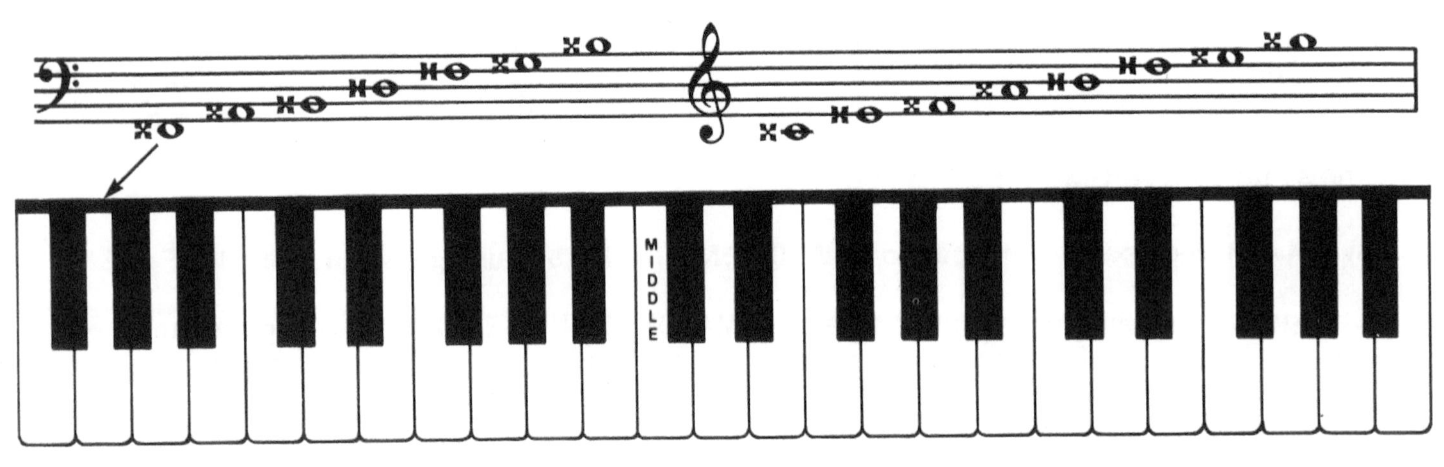

2. The chords in the MAJOR TRIAD column below are spelled correctly. Add SHARPS or DOUBLE SHARPS, when they are needed, to the 3rd or 5th of each chord in the AUGMENTED TRIAD column, so that each 3rd is a MAJOR 3rd above the root, and each 5th is an AUGMENTED 5th above the root.

MAJOR TRIADS			AUGMENTED TRIADS		
Root	3rd	5th	Root	3rd	5th
C	E	G	C	E	G
G	B	D	G	B	D
D	F♯	A	D	F	A
A	C♯	E	A	C	E
E	G♯	B	E	G	B
B	D♯	F♯	B	D	F
F♯	A♯	C♯	F♯	A	C
C♯	E♯	G♯	C♯	E	G

3. Play each MAJOR TRIAD, followed by the AUGMENTED TRIAD in the column on the right. Use R.H. 1 3 5 or L.H. 5 3 1, saying the name of each chord as you play it: "C MAJOR, C AUGMENTED," etc.

The Key of E♭ Major

Assign with pages 78–79.

1. Write the letter names of the notes of the E♭ MAJOR SCALE, from *left to right*, on the keyboard below. Be sure the WHOLE STEPS & HALF STEPS are correct!

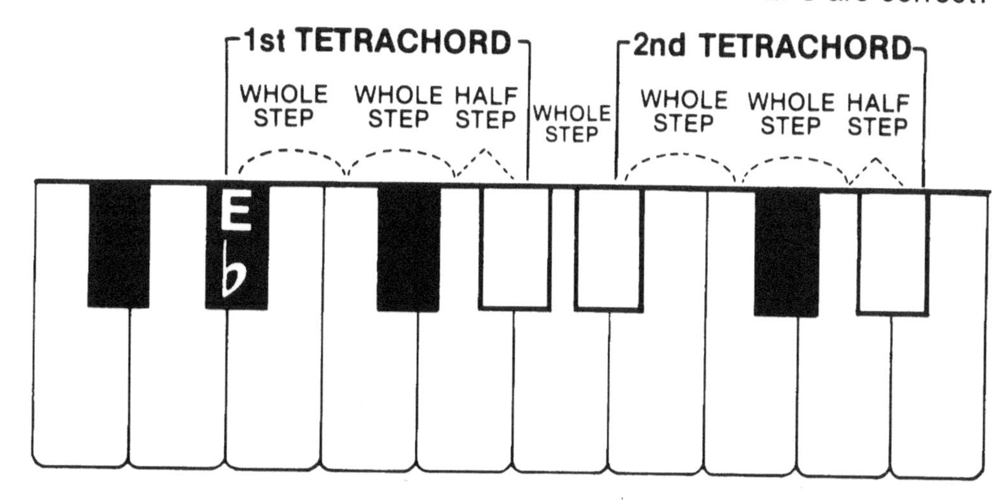

2. Check to be sure that you wrote A♭ as the 4th note of the scale, and B♭ as the 5th note. These notes cannot be called G♯ and A♯, because scale notes must always be named in alphabetical order. (You cannot have two G's and no A's, or two A's and no B's!)

3. Complete the tetrachord beginning on E♭. Write one note over each finger number.

4. Complete the tetrachord beginning on B♭. Write one note over each finger number.

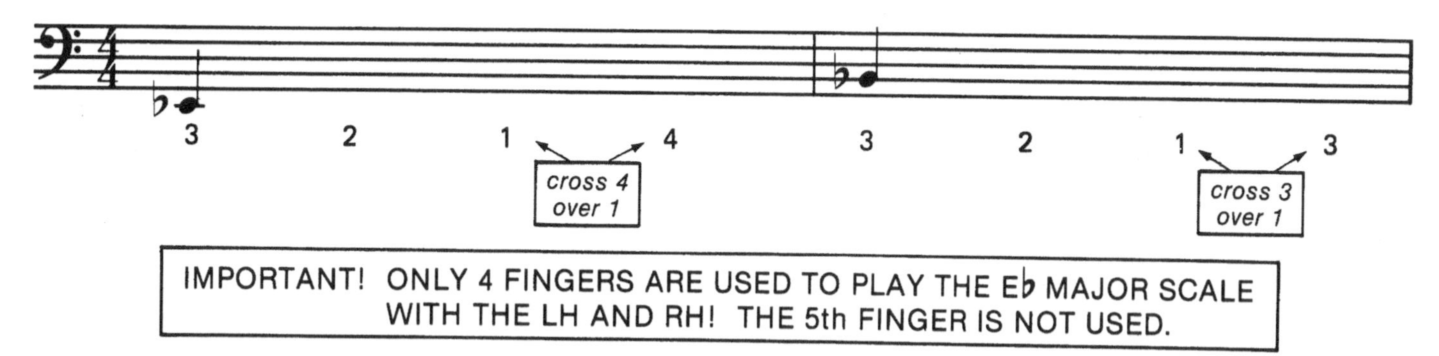

Beginning with LH 3, the scale is fingered in groups of 3 2 1 - 4 3 2 1; end on 3.

5. Write the fingering UNDER each note of the following LH scale.

6. Play with LH.

After beginning with RH 3, the finger groups then fall 1 2 3 4 - 1 2 3.

7. Write the fingering OVER each note of the following RH scale.

8. Play with RH.

Assign with pages 80-81.

The Primary Chords in E♭ Major

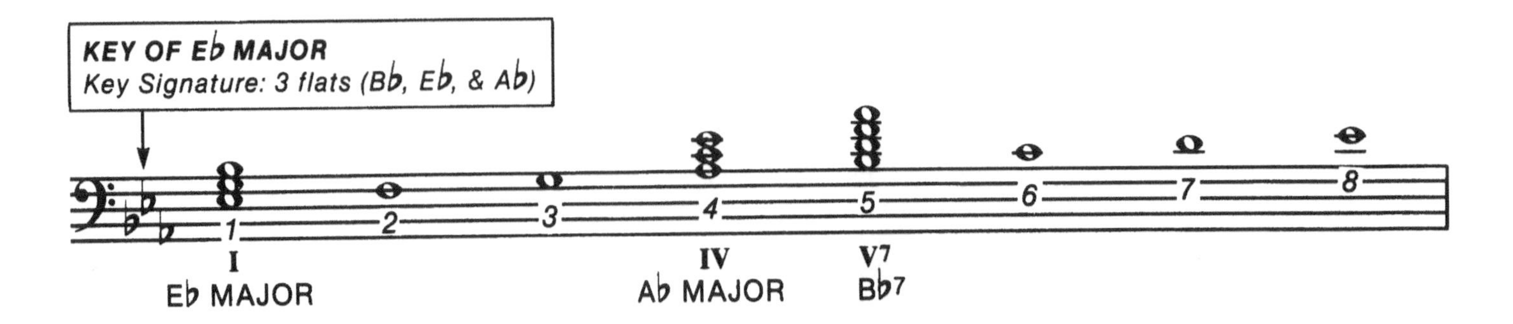

The following positions are often used for smooth progressions:

E♭ is the COMMON TONE between **I** & **IV**. **B♭** is the COMMON TONE between **I** & **V7**.

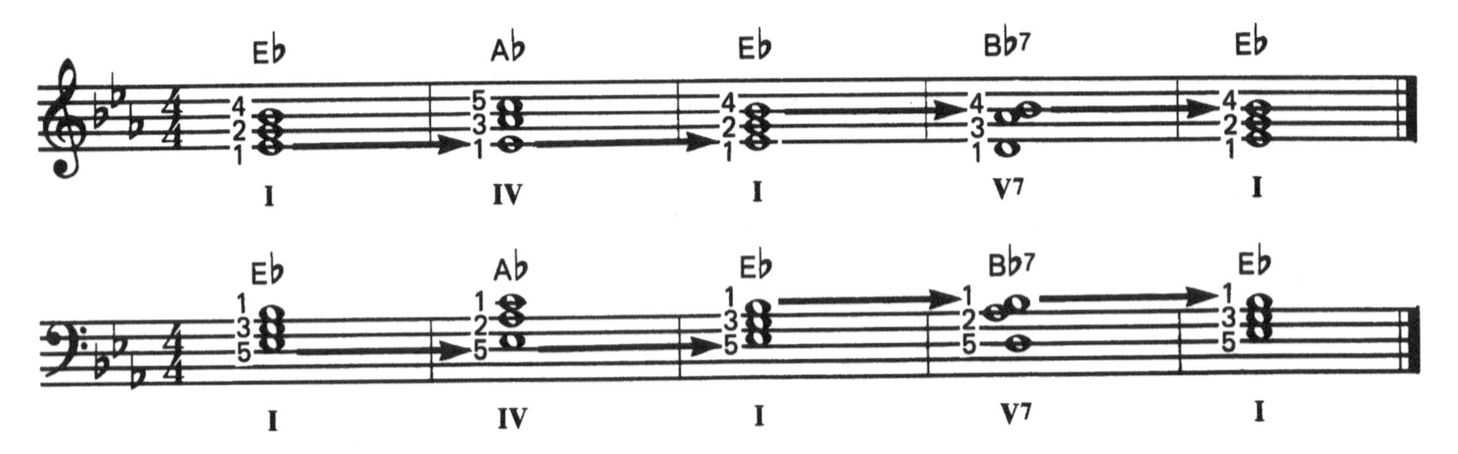

1. Rewrite the above progressions on the following staffs.
2. Add fingering.
3. Add arrows to show the common tones.
4. Play with hands separate.

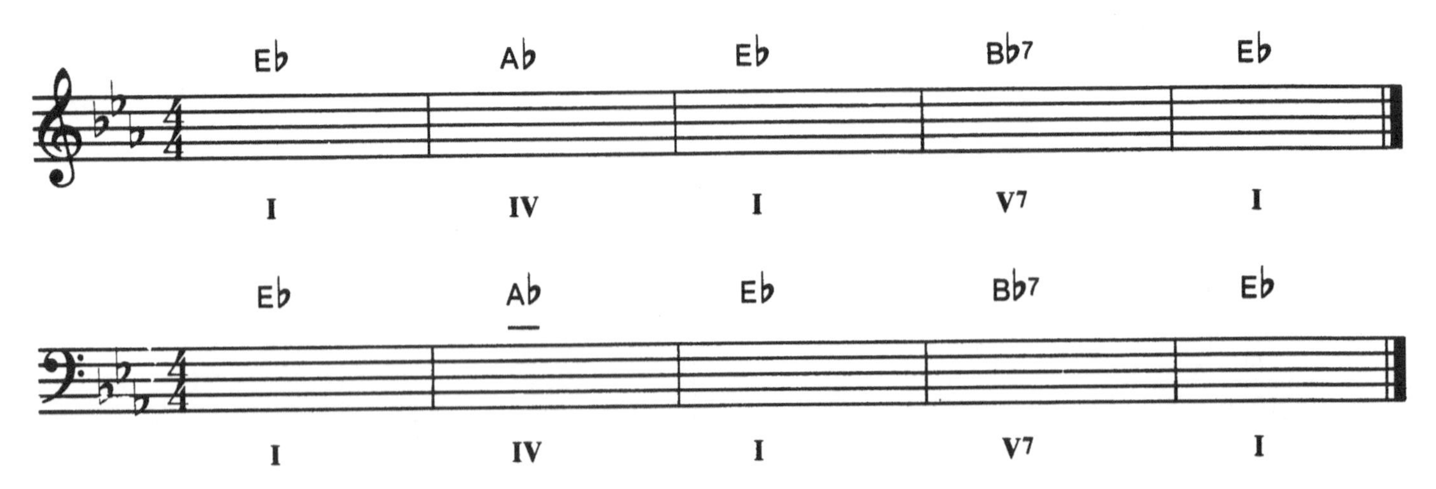

Assign with pages 80–81.

The Primary Chords in E♭ Major—All Positions

1. In the blank measures after each ROOT POSITION chord, write the 2 INVERSIONS of the chord.

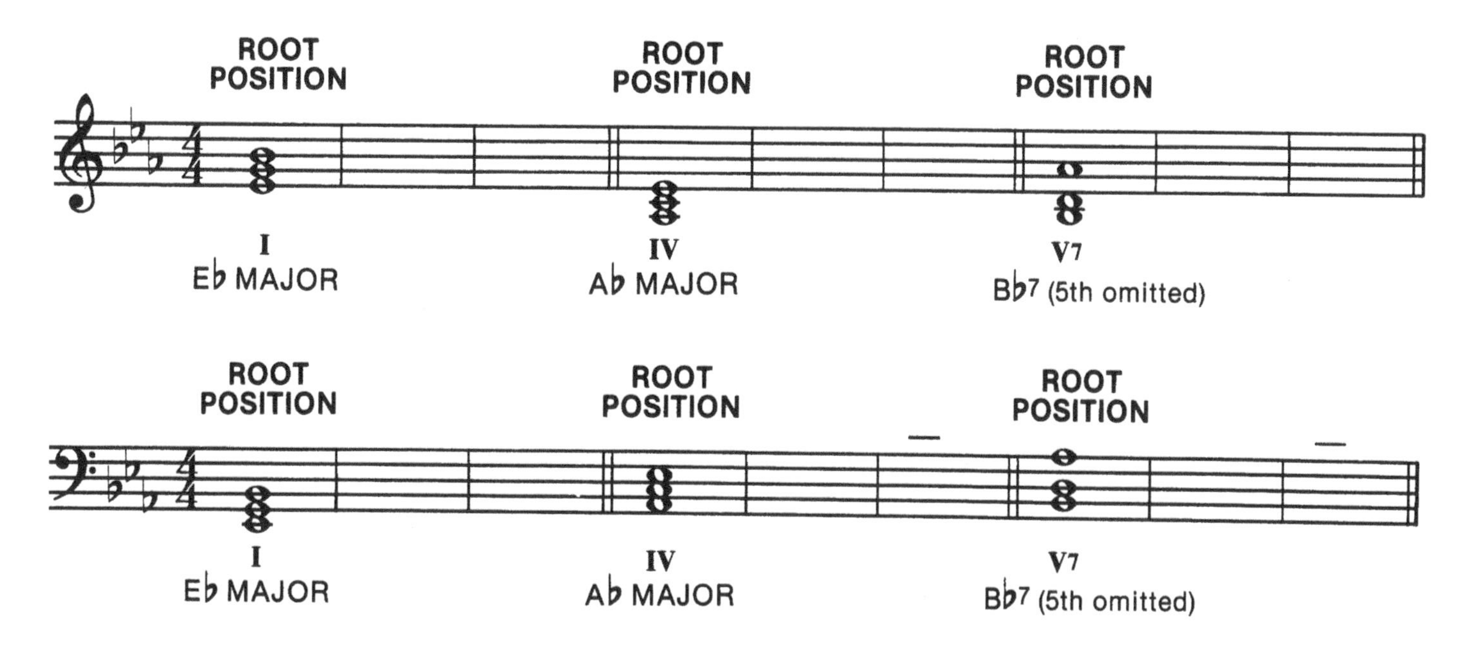

2. On the 2 keyboards to the right of each ROOT POSITION chord, write the letter names showing the 2 inversions of the chord.

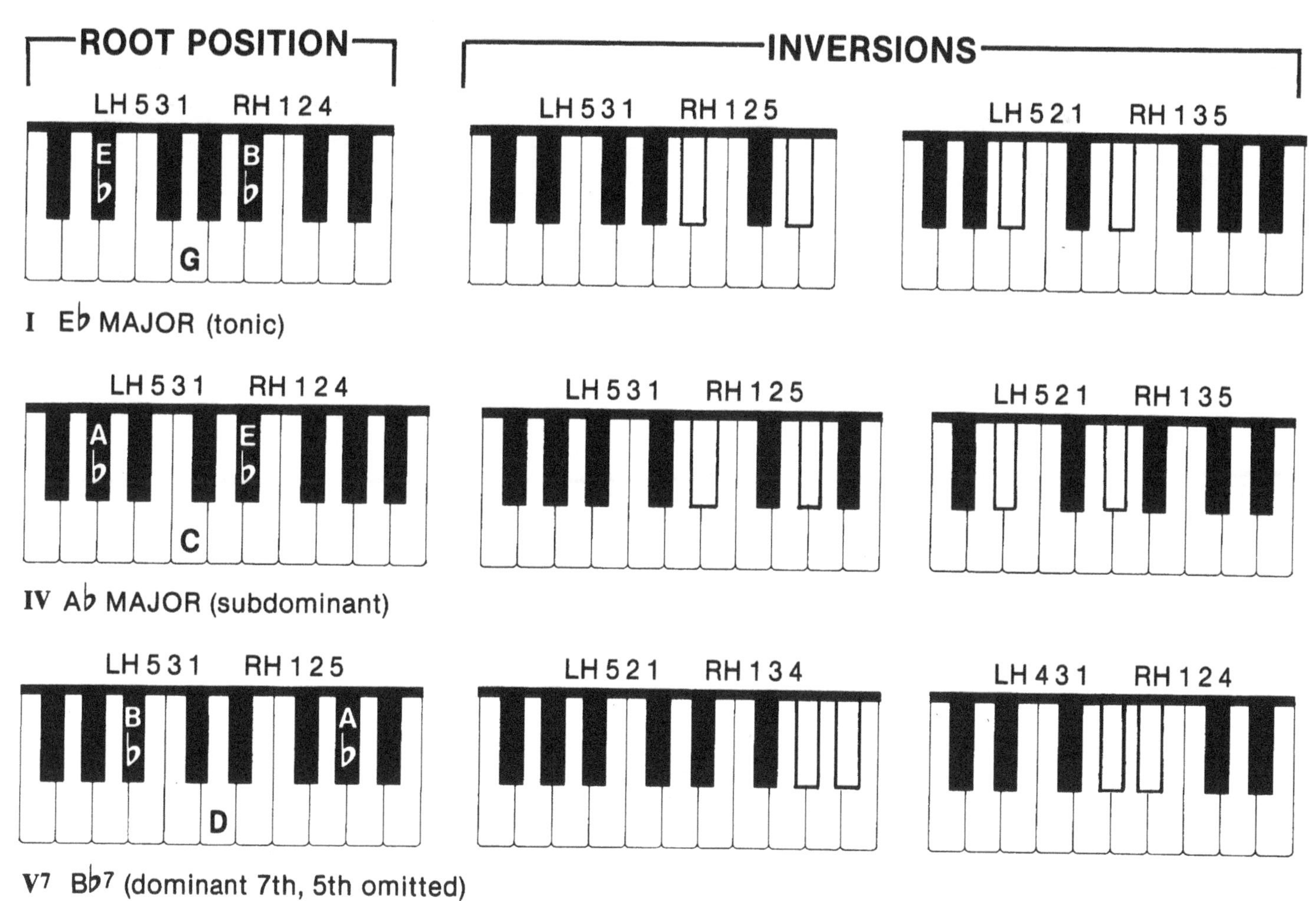

3. Play each chord shown on the above keyboards in any convenient place on your piano, first with LH, then with RH. Use the fingering shown above each keyboard.

Introducing: The Trill

Assign with pages 82–83.

- The TRILL is a rapid alternation of the written note with the note above it.
- The most commonly used signs indicating a trill are: *tr* and *tr*~~~~~~~

The trills in the following piece are played as sixteenth notes, and begin on the note ABOVE the written note. Some are on half notes, and some are on dotted quarter notes.

TRUMPET TUNE

1. In the measure above each trill, write out the notes in full, as shown in the examples above.
2. Play the piece.

Beginning: The Circle of 5ths

Assign with pages 84-87.

The CIRCLE OF 5ths is useful in understanding scales, key signatures, and chord progressions.
The notes of the Circle of 5ths are a PERFECT FIFTH (7 half steps) apart.
The NATURAL NOTES in the circle of 5ths are **F C G D A E B,** moving **CLOCKWISE** around the circle.

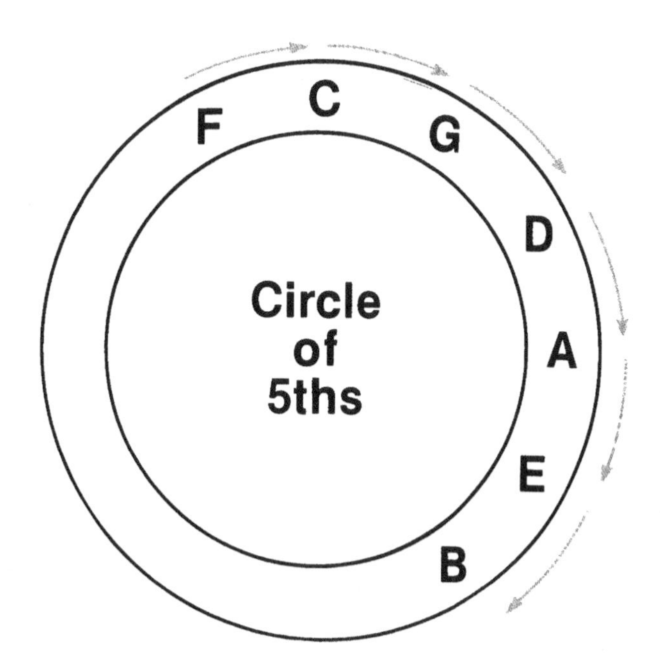

Below are the NATURAL NOTES of the CIRCLE OF 5ths, moving **CLOCKWISE** as they appear on the keyboard.

1. Write a WHOLE NOTE on the staff below for each key indicated on the keyboard, going up the keyboard in PERFECT 5ths. (A PERFECT 5th = 7 HALF STEPS.)
2. Play the notes, using LH or RH 3.

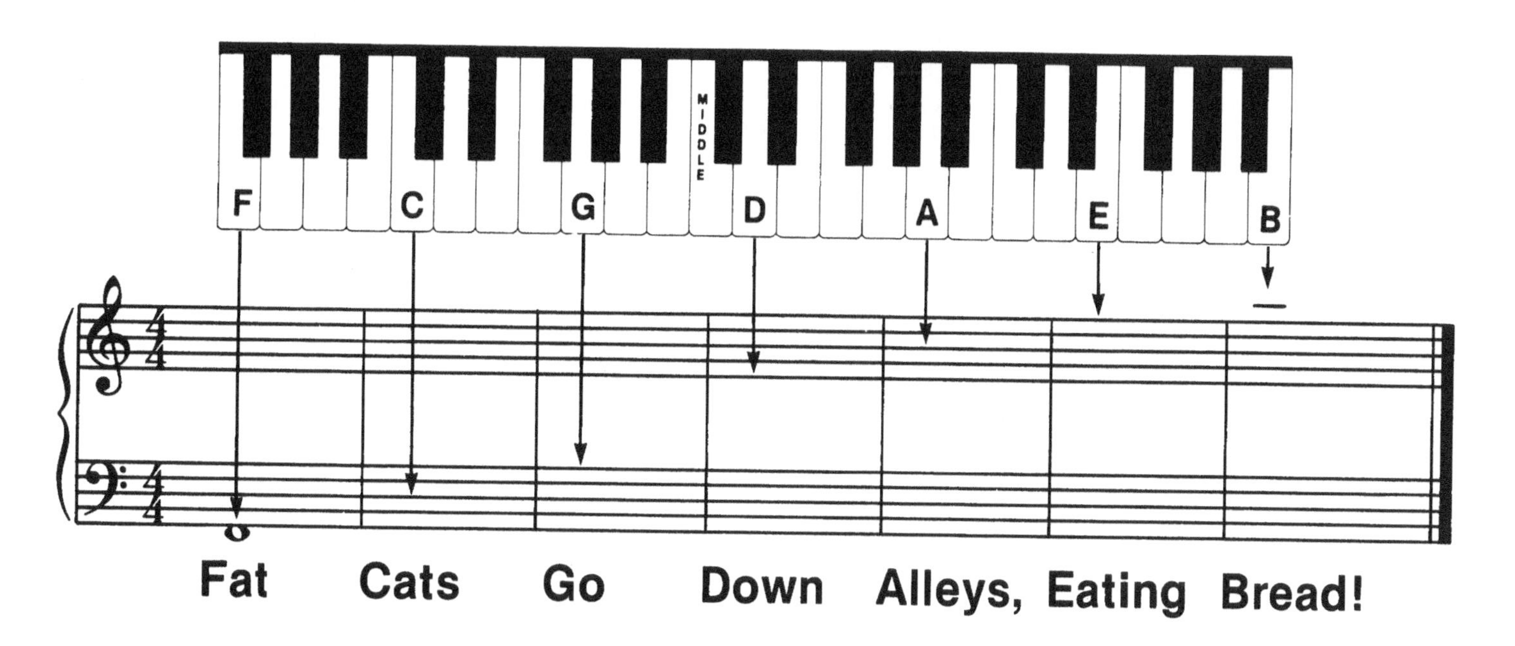

3. MEMORIZE the natural notes of the Circle of 5ths: **F C G D A E B**

Keys Around the Circle of 5ths

Assign with pages 84-87.

1. Build a TETRACHORD on each note indicated on the keyboard below. Write the letter names of the notes of the tetrachords on the keys.

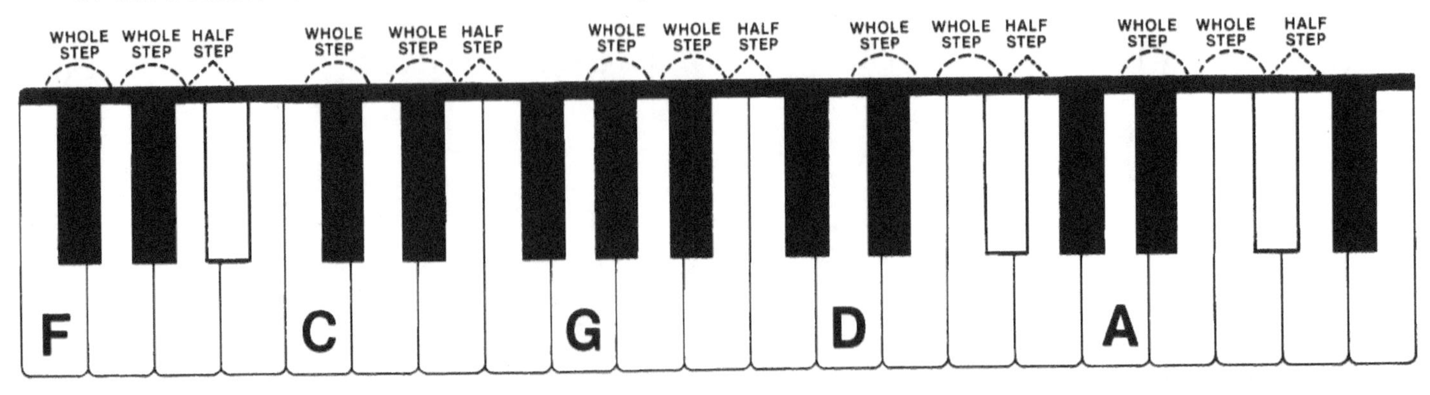

2. Play the above tetrachords in pairs:

The 1st with LH 5 4 3 2 — the 2nd with RH 2 3 4 5.

(1st) **F** — **C** (2nd)
(1st) **C** — **G** (2nd)
(1st) **G** — **D** (2nd)
(1st) **D** — **A** (2nd)

EACH PAIR OF TETRACHORDS MAKES A MAJOR SCALE!

THE KEY SIGNATURES ARE IN THE FOLLOWING ORDER AROUND THE CIRCLE OF 5ths, MOVING CLOCKWISE

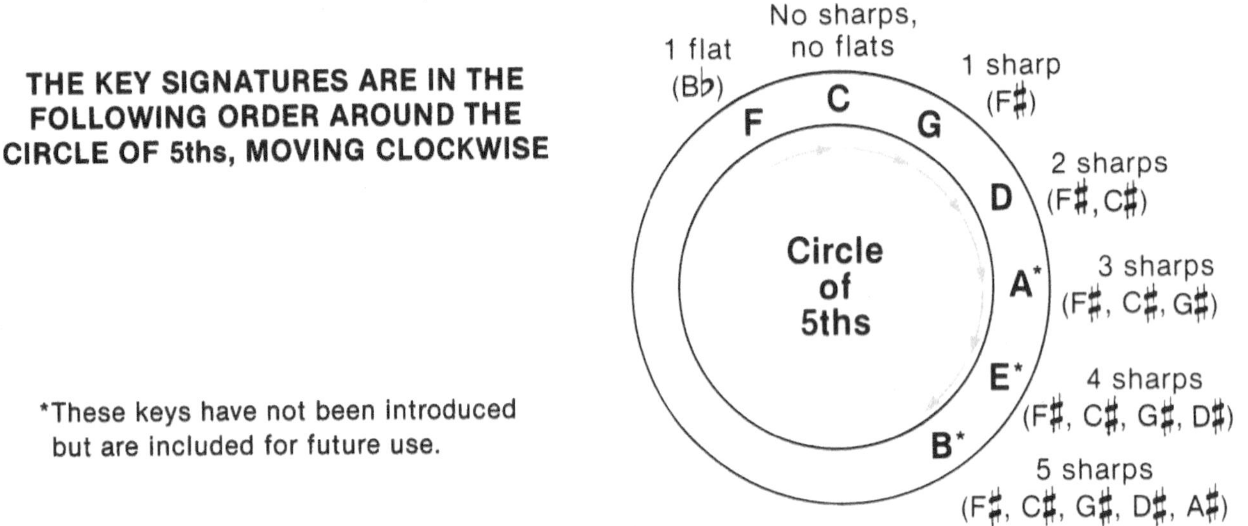

*These keys have not been introduced but are included for future use.

3. Play the following scales with the LH, using the fingering BELOW the notes.
4. Play them with the RH, using the fingering ABOVE the notes.

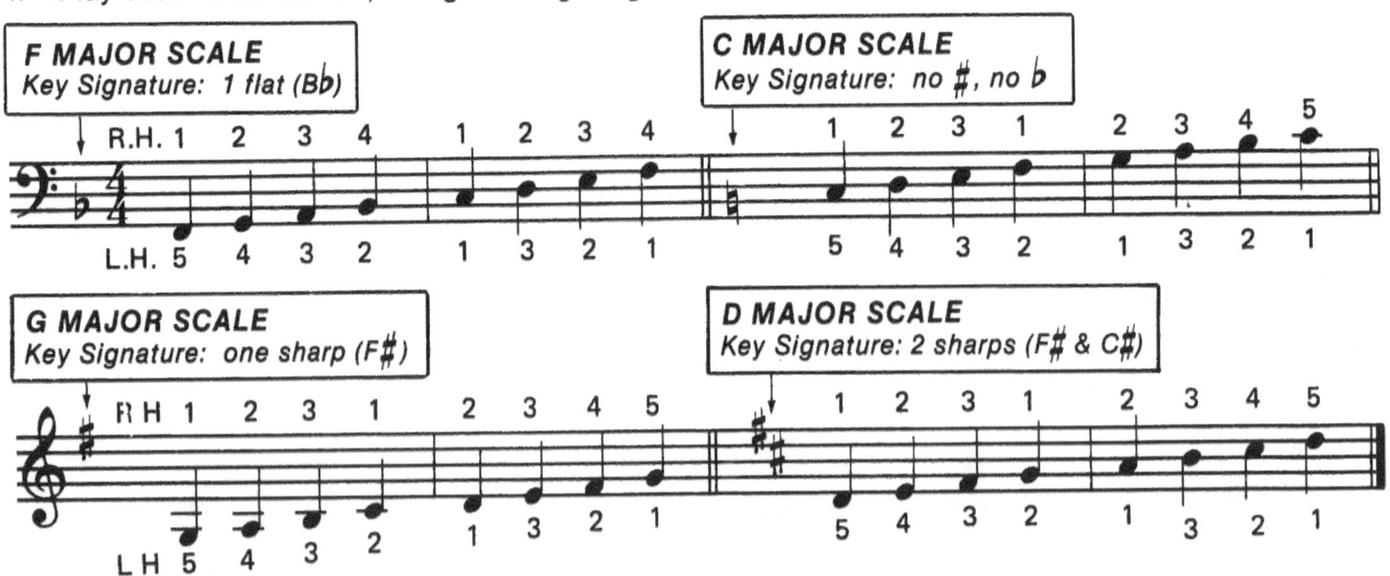

Continuing: The Circle of 5ths

Assign with pages 84-87.

When we move around the CIRCLE OF 5ths **COUNTER-CLOCKWISE** from F, we move through the FLAT KEYS. The notes are a PERFECT FIFTH (7 half steps) APART.

The FLAT NOTES in the Circle of 5ths are **B♭ E♭ A♭ D♭.**

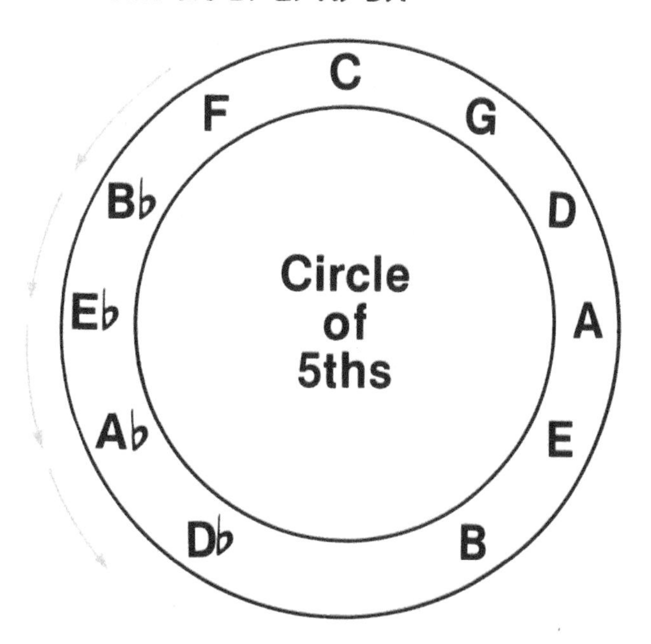

Below are the FLAT NOTES of the CIRCLE OF 5ths, moving **COUNTER-CLOCKWISE,** as they appear on the keyboard:

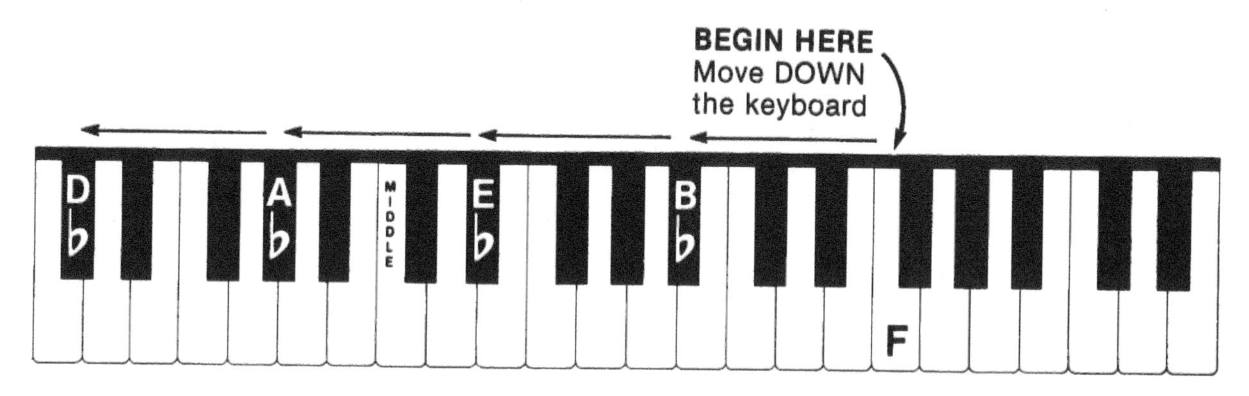

1. Write a WHOLE NOTE on the staff below for each key indicated on the keyboard above, going DOWN the keyboard in PERFECT 5ths. (A PERFECT 5th = 7 HALF STEPS.)
2. Play the notes, using LH or RH.

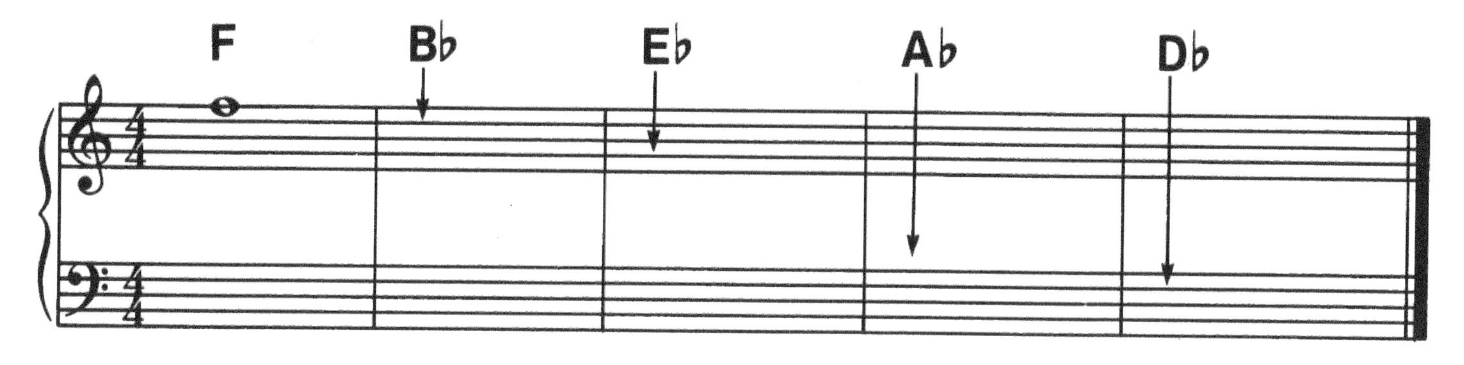

JUST SPELL "B E A D!"

3. **MEMORIZE** the flat notes of the Circle of 5ths: **B♭ E♭ A♭ D♭**

More Keys Around the Circle of 5ths

Assign with pages 84-87.

1. Build a TETRACHORD on each key indicated on the keyboard below. Write the letter names of the notes of the tetrachords on the keys.

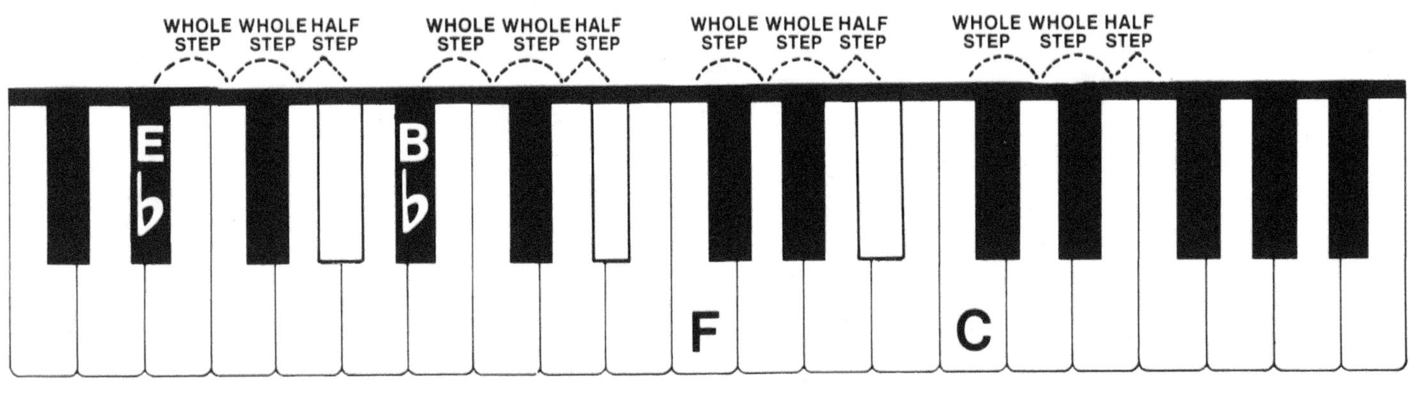

2. Play the above tetrachords in pairs:

The 1st with LH 5 4 3 2 — the 2nd with RH 2 3 4 5.

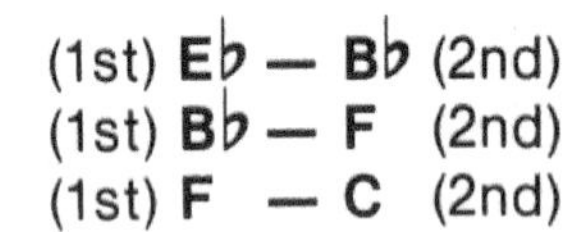

(1st) **E♭ — B♭** (2nd)
(1st) **B♭ — F** (2nd)
(1st) **F — C** (2nd)

EACH PAIR OF TETRACHORDS MAKES A MAJOR SCALE!

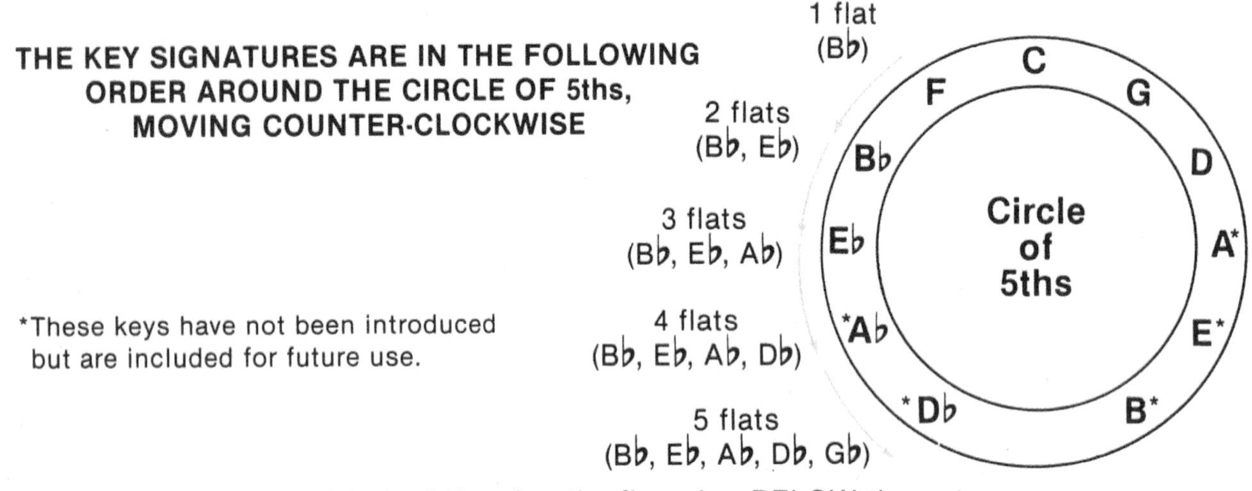

3. Play the following scales with the LH, using the fingering BELOW the notes.
4. Play them with the RH, using the fingering ABOVE the notes.

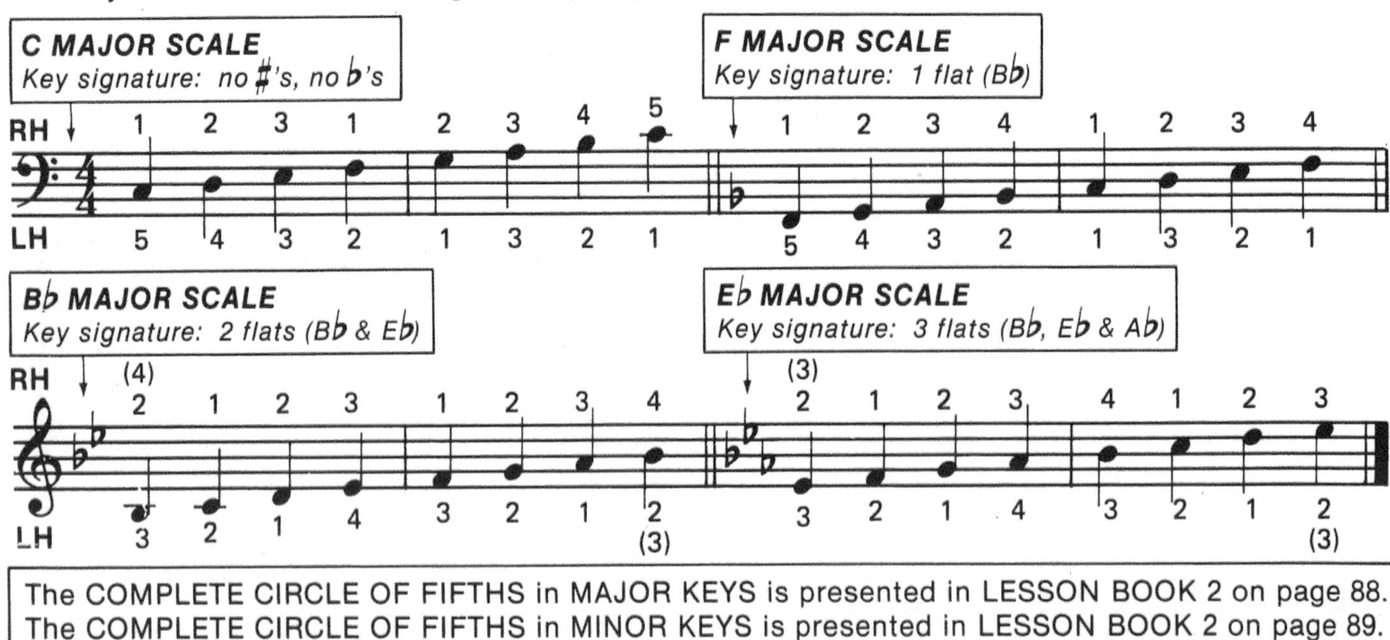

The COMPLETE CIRCLE OF FIFTHS in MAJOR KEYS is presented in LESSON BOOK 2 on page 88.
The COMPLETE CIRCLE OF FIFTHS in MINOR KEYS is presented in LESSON BOOK 2 on page 89.